Strategic Brand Engagement

Strategic Brand Engagement

Using HR and marketing to connect your brand, customers, channel partners and employees

All the best

John G Fisher

KoganPage

LONDON PHILADELPHIA NEW DELHI

First published in Great Britain and the United States in 2014 by Kogan Page Limited

2nd Floor, 45 Gee Street	1518 Walnut Street, Suite 1100	4737/23 Ansari Road
London EC1V 3RS	Philadelphia PA 19102	Daryaganj
United Kingdom	USA	New Delhi 110002
www.koganpage.com		India

© John G Fisher, 2014

The right of John G Fisher to be identified as the author of this work has been asserted by him in accordance with the Copyright, Designs and Patents Act 1988.

ISBN   978 0 7494 7013 5
E-ISBN   978 0 7494 7014 2

British Library Cataloguing-in-Publication Data

A CIP record for this book is available from the British Library.

Library of Congress Cataloging-in-Publication Data

Fisher, John G.
  Strategic brand engagement : using HR and marketing to connect your brand customers, channel partners and employees / John G. Fisher.
     pages cm
  ISBN 978-0-7494-7013-5 (pbk.) – ISBN 978-0-7494-7014-2 (ebk)   1. Corporate culture.
2. Branding (Marketing)   3. Organizational behavior.   4. Personnel management.   I. Title.
  HD58.7.F572 2013
  658.8'27–dc23

                                                                            2013028707

Typeset by Graphicraft Limited, Hong Kong
Printed and bound in Great Britain by CPI Group (UK) Ltd, Croydon, CR0 4YY

CONTENTS

ACKNOWLEDGEMENTS

Authors always stand on the shoulders of others to produce their own books. I would like to thank the following people for their specific help, input and contributions of all kinds in the production of this one: Chris Bestley, Institute of Promotional Marketing; Bruce Bolger, Enterprise Engagement Alliance; The Conyngham Group; Professor Adrian Furnham, UCL; Charlie Griffiths, Stonor Recruitment; David Radford, Allianz; Karen Sharpe, LV=; Allan Schweyer, Human Capital Institute; Dick Stroud, 20 Plus 30 Consulting; Chris Taylor, FMI Group. This list does not include all the people I had conversations with who did not realize at the time they were helping me with the book.

Any misunderstandings, errors and misinterpretations, however, are entirely my own.

Introduction

The use of the written term 'employee engagement', according to Google Analytics, has overtaken phrases such as staff incentives and employee motivation for the first time since 1920. (ENTERPRISE ENGAGEMENT ALLIANCE *BULLETIN*, MARCH 2011)

Engagement is not just for employees

'Brand', 'enterprise' and 'corporate engagement' are relatively new terms that describe the many attempts by organizations to encourage their employees to think favourably about them. The aim is to create improved profits through more loyalty, better efficiency and a 'can do' attitude. Most books and studies about engagement tend to make the general assumption that engagement is something you only do with employees.

In the UK the government raised the issue of employee engagement on a formal basis in 2009 through a paper entitled 'Engage for Success'. Part of the brief was to try and establish a definition of engagement, one of which is shown in the following box.

A positive attitude held by the employee towards the organization and its values. An engaged employee is aware of the business context and works with colleagues to improve business performance within the job for the benefit of the organization. The organization must work to develop and nurture engagement which requires a two-way communication between employee and employer.

The way to do this is to measure your employer/employee interaction using the following four 'enablers':

1 Visible, empowering leadership providing a strong strategic narrative about the organization, where it's come from and where it's going.

2 Engaging managers who focus their people and give them scope, treat their people as individuals and coach and stretch them.

3 Employee voice throughout the organization, for reinforcing and challenging views, between functions and externally; employees are seen as central to the solution.

4 Organizational integrity – the values are reflected in day-to-day activity. There is no 'say – do' gap.

But what about your consumers and your distributors or channel partners? Without consumers employees have no work to engage in. What about distribution, whether we mean your own employed sales people or channel partners? Without channel sales, there would be no products for consumers to buy. Distributors are probably in day-to-day contact more often with your consumers and retail customers than your employees. They play a vital role in bringing your goods to your eventual markets, so they need to be fully engaged with your brand.

Most engagement programmes pay only lip-service to consumers, sellers and channel partners under the guise of 'the brand'. The finer subtleties of brand values are often ignored. That said, large organizations do not make things easy for third parties as the rules for including or not using the organization's name varies greatly and often there is no discernible logic to its inclusion or exclusion. In the same way, channel partners are often signed up or involved at the last moment with engagement programmes, with little thought given to any kind of alignment with what the organization is trying to achieve long-term, except for financial or contractual terms.

Brand alignment with your values and the way the organization deals with the world and its business partners makes for more efficient policies and procedures which, overall, saves money and time for all. There is no need to guess what each should do in any given situation because the brand tells you.

Urgent need to align engagement activities

Why bother to align employee engagement with consumers or channel partners? Because 'push strategies' such as advertising, PR and promotion are limited by the amount you can afford to spend in a crowded and ever more fragmented media market. No brand can keep spending all the time in every medium.

The ideal starting point would be to create the engagement programme alongside the consumer brand and the distribution marketing plan. In other words, when the organization is devising its overall brand and the ways it should be communicated, there should be equally heated debate about how employees and the channel get to know about the brand and what it is supposed to convey in terms of values. If all the people who eventually see and work with your brand are in the picture, and it is the same picture, its uniqueness and consistency will translate into easier sales and profitability.

The logic is compelling, but the reality of organizational politics is such that right now engagement programmes are either HR-led or marketing-led. HR deals with employees and in general marketing deals with channel partners and the consumer brand. Both approaches have merit. But neither function can do the whole job without some key issues remaining unaddressed, so having the work of creating and running the engagement strategy with all your audiences in one place within one business function makes sense. Your organizational brand should not be owned entirely by the marketing team and neither should people policies be solely the prerogative of HR.

The problem is that most organizations are hard-wired to deliver service messages to their employees via the HR function. Sales messages to distributors, internal and external, are usually delivered via the marketing or sales functions. Typically there is very little day-to-day consultation between these two teams. The result is that well-researched, painstaking work on organizational values can be completely undermined by brash and shallow marketing communication, or clever, target-marketed brand imagery can be ignored by the teams that design, service and distribute the goods to consumers. The further complication of a distribution chain with its own multiple brand identities within its own value chain simply adds to the engagement confusion.

The mismatch is relatively easy to fix, but it does require some corporate rewiring to ensure that C-suite level engagement strategy is successfully carried out by staff and distributors in a consistent fashion and that they, as well as consumers, engage with the brand on a level platform with the same values and messages. This means that HR should talk in depth and on a regular basis with marketing, and vice versa, so that they both understand that effective engagement is now a team game.

The components of enterprise engagement

It all starts with the brand. In many organizations this is a 'given' that has been handed down by the perceptions of customers, the owners and employees or is simply the result of history for 'heritage brands'. It may not even be written down in any formal way. Sometimes a new brand has to be developed and created following amalgamations and reconstructions or more likely the appointment of a new CEO. But whether it is formally agreed or not, every organization has a brand, and to be effective employers and employees need to understand what the brand is and how the organization can use brand perception as a way to be more commercially successful.

Alignment with the values of the brand is the traditional way organizations go about streamlining their service to consumers. For example, if their values include providing exceptional service compared with other similar suppliers this will be highlighted in their advertising claims and general promotional offers, possibly in the form of a 'no quibble guarantee' or similar expression that suggests they are a decent and reasonable provider. But few organizations align their brand with their employees, or if they do it is patchy and sometimes unprofessional. How many times have you been seduced by a promotional claim only to find that when you come to complain about the product the after-sales department seems unaware of what the brand promise was. Better alignment at all touch points means better engagement.

Brand: marketing

When the organization has decided how it will go about creating and developing its services and products, market research is often conducted to determine what consumers expect in terms of product, price, promotion and distribution. This is the classic marketing plan. But the principles of corporate engagement now require the plan to be consistent with the organization's values and ethics of both personal and commercial behaviour. So the brand needs to be checked against what employees and distributors feel about the organization. Saying it is not the same as doing it, as many financial services enterprises have learnt to their considerable cost in recent years. Everyone needs to be clustered around the core values.

Vision and values: HR

The mission may well be to create or continue to create particular services within specific markets. But the organization now has to decide how it is going to do that with the employees it has and its current channel partner's network. The first 'how' is to lay down what the values of the organization actually are in practice. This will then determine who to recruit, the expectations of their performance, their work ethics, appraising their performance and their alignment with the overall master brand. To establish true engagement one of the values should be to encourage employee input into the employer brand and its values, turning the traditional approach to strategy on its head. Share, not tell; bottom up, not top down.

Communicating the employer brand: HR

Values and brand need to be communicated to all staff in a consistent manner to echo what B2B/organizational partners and consumers will experience. So, not only does the material have to 'look right' it needs to be fully embedded in the corporate culture through briefing workshops, intranet sites, public areas, private staff areas, recognition systems and staff handbooks.

Research has shown that providing a pictorial map of how the individual employee fits into the overall plan is often better understood than written documents, bar charts and slogans. But all this needs to start with employee involvement at the outset, not simply delegated downwards by a busy senior team with half an eye on the next quarterly numbers.

Sales teams and channel communication: marketing

All sales communication for the internal sales team needs to be 'branded' and tell the same story as is told to the consumer. The same branding and story has to be applied to all channel partner materials with slight variations for wholesalers and retailers in the distribution chain, paying careful attention to the relevant strengths of the business relationships. Sales incentives and preferred supplier deals are often tactical in nature by definition, but they should always align with the vision and values of the promoter. Misalignment breeds confusion.

Employee recognition and non-cash rewards: HR

Compliance with the values of the organization can be strengthened by formal recognition of above-average teams and individual performances on a regular basis, not just at the end of the year. Desired attitudes and performance in the workplace can be further enhanced by non-cash rewards for new ideas and incentives on a tactical basis to ensure that compliance is constantly adjusted to the maximum.

Employee feedback: HR

Employee motivation and morale should be monitored so that brand communications can be fine-tuned on a regular basis. Online surveys, appraisals and workshops provide invaluable insights into performance throughout the organization, and 'engagement gaps' can be quickly highlighted, defined and closed up. Launch-it-and-leave-it is not an option if you want true engagement. Don't rely on annual employee surveys as by the time they are collated and published it will be too late. Your intranet provides you with many opportunities to sample feelings and attitudes in much shorter time intervals.

Sales teams and channel feedback: marketing

Most organizations have many tools to track sales but few monitor the level of engagement within the sales function or third-party channel partners. They often have a different relationship with the organization to normal salaried staff; they certainly behave differently. Identifying mismatches in sales or channel performance and values and taking remedial action can improve sales volume or can identify reasons for any shortfall long before more traditional 'rear-view mirror' techniques reveal performance problems.

Measuring corporate engagement: HR and marketing

As with all business processes, someone somewhere will eventually ask how things are going. Engagement represents a mix of activities that are traditionally not measured with a single index – but they could be. In terms of a dashboard for the stakeholders and owners it is always useful to track top level numbers for engagement on a regular basis, or compare that number with other similar businesses and benchmark performance against this vital factor for organizational success. This could easily extend to distributor measures and customer satisfaction scores from consumers. The dashboard approach, perhaps with different dashboards for each part of the organization, helps managers and team leaders identify specific issues quickly rather than feel dissatisfied with a big overall number.

Social media for organizations: HR and marketing

Technology changes society, organizations and commercial life. Sometimes it seems every new advance will change the way we all operate but few have done so in dramatic ways. Social media is different. A devastating combination of internet connectivity and better mobile devices has resulted in a completely new way of communicating between individuals, both on a personal and a business level. The trouble is the Baby Boomers who mostly run organizations may have just missed out on this medium, leaving many organizations dealing with Generation Y employees on Facebook and everyone else stuck on e-mail. For true employee engagement to happen in a single organization we all need to be on the same platform and using the same shared media.

Do we need a VP of engagement?

Someone has to be in charge of what to do. The buck has to stop somewhere. If the CEO is a hands-off sort of person when it comes to internal processes, will it be HR or marketing that makes the running? If the CEO is hands-on, he or she will still need to decide at various stages of the engagement process whether we go with what marketing says or what HR says. What is really needed is an 'engagement VP' to give equally-weighted guidance to both functions.

It is not often that there is the opportunity to change the old way of doing things and take advantage of new insights. Employing an engagement VP may be the answer. True corporate or organizational engagement brings together HR people-development models with marketing and communication skills under one banner. What's more, it is a measure that consumers and media commentators can understand and respond to. In the years to come it will be viewed as an obvious improvement for all successful organizations to have made. Future commentators will no doubt chuckle to themselves that until the 21st century most large organizations deliberately split the strategic task of engagement between two or more departments with the inevitable misalignment and lack of mutual accountability. Now that we have, or could have, engagement VPs the big divide between HR and marketing will become an oddity of the past.

Integrated engagement fits all sizes

Before we begin though, here's a personal word to readers who do not work for a well-known brand or multinational conglomerate. Statistically speaking, most of us don't.

Apple, Google, Microsoft and Toyota, for example, are, by all accounts, very effective organizations. But how applicable are their global lessons for a small engineering company trying to make ends meet in a static, local market? If you want to know how 'big organizations' attempt to fix the engagement gap, there is a bibliography at the back of this book, which I would encourage you to consult. The books are well-written and explain in detail what the specific issues with large organizations were and how they were fixed. But they are at best temporary snapshots of specific situations, not a panacea for all engagement ills across all markets for all types of organization. Economies and markets change, it seems, more quickly than they used to, which suggests that engagement strategies may need to change too. It can be off-putting as a smaller enterprise to read about global organizations with huge resources that can do things like peer group benchmarking without having to think about the cost. But the principles are the same. Nothing will be lost by implementing even local programmes of recognition or employee involvement in supporting brand values beyond the immediate organization. Engagement works, even for local firms.

In this book I am not claiming that there is a silver bullet. I am simply hoping to share best practice rather than *prove* best practice from both HR and marketing disciplines. My aim is that you will find many ideas that you could implement in your own organization immediately or within the next planning cycle to improve engagement. When I read business books I often find that one apparently unrelated idea or example sparks a thought about a completely different part of an organization which I had not considered before or was even seeking out. If any part of this book provokes an improvement, however small, it will have done its job.

This book is written in a sequence that mirrors how you might go about overhauling your current approach to brand engagement. It can be read as a strategic primer to guide you through the project. If you have never tackled engagement before, I hope this will help to clarify your thoughts as to where to start. Equally, if you are an established brand or are looking to implement or fine-tune an agreed strategy you can afford to skip through the bits you have already done. Particular chapters may be useful in isolation, if you have come across a specific issue that your team needs to resolve in order to move forward, or you might want to revisit some old issues within your current engagement process to look for improvements.

No one gets it right all the time, no matter how many consultants you may have employed or how long you have been doing it. A change of ownership or leadership can quickly alter the dynamics of employee and channel engagement in a significant way, so 'same again, please' may no longer be an option for you.

My final plea is to ask you to suspend your natural scepticism that marketing does not understand its own employees and that HR is hopeless at communicating and dealing with sales people or the channel. None of this is true… all of the time. In fact I have found that marketing people have deep insights into what employees really think. After all, they are employees themselves. HR people are acutely aware of what makes for an effective message, because they are themselves on the receiving end of messages from marketing or internal communications all the time. They may even see those messages in the public domain, if they work for a well-known organization. The problem is that HR and marketing just don't talk to each other enough to become real experts in the specific disciplines of their corporate partners. If they were to engage more regularly with each other, to use the jargon, the bottom-line result would be more effective, more brand-aligned and more profitable overall for their organization.

One frustration I find sometimes with business books is trying to get in contact with the author, either to agree or disagree or simply to clarify. The rise in social media means people now expect to have direct dialogue with those who are prepared to put opinions into the public domain. For that reason I have included my direct business e-mail address below.

If you work for a famous brand, I hope you will enjoy the insights from all types of organizations, big and small, and learn about how differently your counterparts in marketing or HR may see the same corporate world you inhabit. If you don't work for a world leader, please do read on. This book is mainly for you and about you and your more local struggle to get engagement issues on the strategic agenda to help improve performance, profits and employee involvement.

John Fisher, Oxford, 2013
John.fisher@fmigroup.co.uk

What is strategic brand engagement?

01

> *In order to make and keep that (the brand's) promise an organization's internal branding and external brand expression must be two sides of the same coin.*
>
> **(WOLFGANG GHIEL AND JOSEPH LEPLA, 2012)**

Everything in business seems to be strategic these days. Business plans, new initiatives, advertising campaigns and acquisitions are often reported in the media and by organizations themselves as being 'strategic'. It begs the question as to what we mean by the word.

Defining strategic

Strategos is a Greek word meaning a military general. So you could say strategy means what a general does in war. He plans military action. He assesses the enemy's position and resources, examines his own resources and considers variables such as the weather, the environment and his supply lines. He positions his troops and resources to overcome the enemy with as little loss of life as possible.

In business, strategy is usually taken to mean the overarching plan to achieve a goal with a similar regard to minimizing losses, but in this case they would be financial. So a multinational's strategy could be to adapt its successful domestic market products and processes to suit various niche markets, internationally. A local retailer's strategy could be to offer basic products at cheaper prices than its competitors. A charity's strategy could be to help fund research to cure a debilitating disease. Chandler, back in the 1960s, defined commercial strategy as 'the determination of the basic long-term goals and objectives of an enterprise, and the adoption of courses of action and the allocation of resources necessary for carrying out these goals'.

So, a strategy is the research and creation of a plan. It is not the implementation of the plan itself. It is not the meticulous detail that characterizes operational processes or promotional activity. It is not the measurement of all the minutiae that characterizes many of the tasks that make up daily life in human resources or marketing. Delivering the plan could best be described as the 'tactics'. The distinction is important because there is a tendency in most organizations to rush forward to agreeing tactics – we could do this, we could do that, we could copy them – before determining fully what the goals for their own enterprise are and whether, if they go ahead and do something quickly, they will actually like the result. Be careful what you wish for is often good advice. The more time you spend determining what outcome you want, the more you will like what you eventually get.

Igor Ansoff's definition of a corporate strategy formulated in the 1960s (*Corporate Strategy*, 1965 and later editions) has not been improved upon in almost 50 years:

1 Provides a broad concept of the firm's business.
2 Sets forth specific guidelines by which the firm can conduct its search (for new opportunities).
3 Supplements the firm's objectives with decision rules.

In this context he was talking about acquisition and growth but apply these thoughts to brand engagement and you have the definition of strategy in a simple format that sets out general values of the organization, provides signposts for better engagement and presents all employees and other stakeholders with general rules by which engagement can be pursued.

Strategy also needs to be competitive with peer organizations. These days almost all sector data is available online. It therefore comes as no surprise that for large organizations strategy can sometimes seem to be nothing new or different. If everyone has done their desk research effectively the strategy for a similar size corporation in the same sector with the same global reach, give or take a few countries, comes up with remarkably similar answers. The skill is to then assess what your unique quality is and how you can take advantage of that uniqueness to leverage better performance.

As Michael Porter (2004) says: 'Competitive strategy is about being different. It means deliberately choosing a different set of activities to deliver a unique mix of value.' It may well be that your approach to engagement is the thing that differentiates your organization from other similar size competitors and becomes the turnkey reason why you outperform the market when everyone else is just 'doing the numbers'.

A common mistake is to use the words 'strategy' and 'tactics' interchangeably as if they mean the same thing. If we return to its Greek roots, 'tactics' describes the actual lines of battle a general draws up or his deployment of troops to achieve the battle plan. In other words, tactics are the detailed actions and activities that need to be undertaken to achieve the end goal. For an insurance company a tactic could be to offer reduced rates for multiple car cover in order to sell more policies to the same customer. An airline might invest in more comfortable seats to attract more of the business market. A school could offer online learning resources to help pupils who are not able to get to classes for whatever local reason. These are all tactics. So, when we talk about strategic brand engagement we are laying down the principles of how an organization, any organization, should set about planning to communicate and influence all its possible audiences with its brand values, not just consumers, not just employees and not just channel partners.

Tactical brand engagement, for example, would include all the minutiae of how to run a focus group, what media to use for communication, how to measure engagement in detail and what actual words to use in employee and distributor briefings. You can imagine how these would be very different depending on the audiences involved and the market situation. It is unlikely that you would use the same tone of voice with your consumers, your channel partners and your employees. For one thing your terms of employment with employees and of business with channel partners are completely different so your capacity to leverage compliance from them varies.

No single learning resource could provide for all the variables you would need to consider for the tactics of specific engagement with every audience you ever have dealings with. However, when you embrace fully the concept of brand engagement, the tactical skills and techniques you need will fall into place. You will not need a reference book to come up with them. They will appear from the research and planning that you do and be completely relevant to your organization at the time you are implementing them.

They key thing at the beginning of your engagement journey is therefore the *strategic* approach to brand engagement where time spent planning is time well spent. Don't worry too much about the tactics for now.

Defining your brand

Most, but not all, marketing people understand that a brand is much more than a logo or a trademark, but many consumers and non-marketing employees do not. This will be explored in more detail in Chapter 3, but for now let's make some broad statements.

An organization's brand is an expression of a product or service promise. It could even be a guarantee of quality. It often includes a set of shared differences that sets your organization apart from every other organization in the world. You have a unique history and a unique team of employees, even if you have only been trading for a few years or even a few months. Many historically successful organizations, sometimes known as 'heritage brands', have established over time such a strong reputation that new employees and suppliers to that organization already have an expectation of how they will be treated by that organization because of its historic brand values. This set of values is probably only known in detail by a handful of internal executives but experienced by all those who have dealings with the organization.

Typically a heritage brand (organization) will be perceived as being 'authentic' in that it has a real history of dealing with consumers over many decades – or centuries in a few cases. It is obvious what it does, it treats consumers fairly and, being in the public domain it is often openly accountable to many national and international institutions such as government bodies, trade associations and, most important, public opinion. Consumers buy from it because they know exactly what they will get in terms of quality of service and value for money. By extension all these attributes need to be supported internally at all their touch points with consumers, from advertising and national sponsorships to administration partners and retail outlets.

Even start-ups have a brand

If you are a relatively new organization you already have a 'brand' even if you have not formally communicated it to anyone. The way you do business is your master brand together with the way you hire and fire employees and contract with suppliers. You will need to define that set of shared values and ways of dealing with internal and external customers before you can begin to improve your engagement with the wider world. This will be enlightening in itself, as it will probably be the first time that anyone has ever expressed what they really think about your organization or how it is perceived beyond the confines of your plant, warehouse or office. You may be surprised to discover that your brand is largely how potential customers are dealt with by e-mail or by phone. That may not be how you see it. But you have to deal with the reality of consumer perceptions rather than how you would like it to be. So 'first touch points' are important indicators of a new brand's perception.

What consumers expect has to be supported by a raft of internal procedures to ensure that the brand delivers on its promise or consumers will simply walk down the road to your direct competitor. That's how capitalism works. So when we talk about the brand we really mean the set of shared values that consumers expect to find when dealing with you and your organization. You can see how maintaining and defending the brand is not just a task for the marketing department – it is every employee's job to do so. By extension it is also every channel partner's job to deliver what consumers expect.

It is clear then that your printed 'logo' or organizational emblem does not mean brand. These are just symbols of the master brand, which is infinitely more complex to define and much more pervasive (see Chapter 3).

Defining engagement

It could be argued that 'engagement' is also a military term. The rules of engagement are a set of procedures armies lay down that determine who to attack, when to attack and with what resources. Within a commercial context 'engagement' has a more mutually beneficial meaning. In general it tends to mean the degree to which audiences will 'go the extra mile' to comply with what the organization requires, in a perfect world.

There are probably in excess of 20 definitions of organizational engagement, all a little bit different depending on your point of view and who needs to know. Some point to a statistical measure, usually expressed as a percentage, of how well-disposed employees are to the organization when asked: 'How engaged do you feel with your employer?' The useful thing about having a figure is that it can be tracked over time so that you can see whether you are doing better or worse than the last time you asked. As an absolute measure by itself it is almost meaningless because you would need to compare the result with other similar organizations, other different organizations or other divisions, perhaps within your own organization.

Some people view engagement as yet another magic formula for managing people successfully. Professor of Psychology, Adrian Furnham, University College London puts it like this: 'The business world is famous for its search for the Holy Grail of management simplicity: the search for a formula (process) which makes the capricious, complex and risky world of managing people easy, straightforward and successful' (private communication, May 2013).

Another approach to defining engagement could be a psychological score for feelings of trust, loyalty, being focused, being enthusiastic, being caring or intensity of feelings. When employees are surveyed, abstract concepts are whittled down to a few pithy statements with which respondents are invited to 'strongly agree or strongly disagree' on a sliding scale.

A third approach could be to build the questions around the already agreed core values of the sponsor and ask how much (or how little) you feel aligned to these values ... and if not, why not. You could certainly measure engagement with reference to a complex, psychological formula, with any variables being introduced for different types of employee or business partner. Professor Furnham again:

> Managers' style and behaviour directly affect employee engagement... that is managers create, sustain or break engagement. Good management practices are set by senior managers who are responsible for strategy, processes and culture. Engagement comes from the top. It is relatively fragile and needs constant attention. (ibid)

Satisfaction is not necessarily engagement

Some organizations use adaptations of tried and tested customer satisfaction survey formats to measure engagement of employees. After all, if they work for customers why wouldn't they work equally well for employees?

The thinking is that if you look after your people and they are 'satisfied' then customers will be satisfied too and therefore this makes the organization successful, financially-speaking. A number of studies have shown that an X per cent increase in employee satisfaction scores can be directly correlated to a Y per cent increase in sales. The problem is that such surveys concentrate on the process rather than intangibles such as enthusiasm and creativity. So you may well have a high score for 'satisfaction' but only in so far as your employees are compliant with existing processes. Employees can only agree or disagree with what they are asked about, when an engagement survey would explore more abstract and emotional issues. An engagement survey should measure enthusiasm, passion and moments of deep connection with the values of the business, not just compliance with pre-determined, best practice processes.

Towards a definition

At this point it may be worth an attempt to provide a definition for future reference as all three words of 'strategic brand engagement', as we have seen, carry a multitude of meanings that are at best easily misunderstood or at worst ignored. My definition is as follows:

> *Strategic brand engagement is the top-line plan that brings together all the elements of an organization's brand and its impact on employees, consumers and channel partners to create a more profitable and sustainable future.*

The key element of this approach is the synergy that can be derived from bringing all three audiences together under one agenda. It is a people issue rather than a promotional or creative one, so attempts to affect the level of brand engagement are to do with audience intervention plans rather than changing the brand image itself.

Starting the engagement journey

The best way to describe what strategic brand engagement is all about is to visualize what it feels like. Strategically engaged employees or channel partners means having a higher than normal number of enthusiastic, positive thinking, pro-organization 'ambassadors' for your brand. It means in the wider world of consumers and the channel that you have a higher than average number of people who are actively involved in improving the way you bring your goods and services to market, thereby assisting in improved consumer or distributor sales.

To be successful at organizational engagement you need to have a plan. Rather than starting with an employee survey or an ideas scheme, you should spend some time defining your values and the expectations of your customers and channel partners. Are your current brand and its perceived values actually something you and they agree with? If it is, fine, off you go with tactical implementation. But I would suspect that there may be a mismatch between what you think your brand is and what they now think it is, especially if such an appraisal has not been undertaken for several years.

You also need to consider what engagement looks like for your specific organization. It could be something intangible, a mixture of opinions, gut feel and rooted in your heritage. Equally it could be strongly linked to a new product or a new CEO. Whatever it is, it is unique, so following a consultant's previous formula is unlikely to deliver what some marketers call the 'delight' factor.

If you are truly embarking on strategic brand engagement you will need to cross-reference what consumers think against what your employees think, with a link to your channel partner brands. The over-arching idea is that, if only you could get alignment and agreement about the shared set of values across all three players in the game (consumers, employees and sellers), then profits will improve because the reasons to buy from you will be compellingly strategic, not just tactically convenient.

The first hurdle to overcome is, of course, the business case for spending resources on engagement. The next chapter provides some useful and persuasive arguments for embarking on a brand engagement strategy.

Why engagement matters

02

"*A study by global services provider Towers Watson found that high-engagement firms experienced an earnings-per-share (EPS) growth rate of 28 per cent, compared with an 11.2 per cent decline for low-engagement firms.*

(ALLAN SCHWEYER, HUMAN CAPITAL INSTITUTE)

We have agreed that for true engagement to work it needs to be strategic – planned for – and needs to be fully aligned with the organization's brand, whatever that now is. But the next question is, why bother? Even though you may feel instinctively that getting more engagement from your employees and the market has to be better than not doing so, there will be a cost involved and does it actually deliver a better bottom line than not doing it at all?

There are many techniques for success that you can use to improve the efficiency of an organization so as to attract more investment, which you need so that you can expand your products and services, either nationally or globally. There has been a tendency to drill ever deeper into the organization to find those essential ingredients for success amongst employees that are specific and unique. As marketing becomes ever blander, particularly for global organizations, an increasingly important factor in assessing future potential by analysts is how well an organization engages with its employees and channel partners or other advocates rather than relying purely on the consumer or product offering. This is particularly valuable with me-too conglomerates that offer the same type of products to the same type of customers.

Traditional methods of improving positive involvement with the overall aims of the organization have had limited success, perhaps moving the engagement score by a few points and then falling back when the internal leadership or learning programme has been withdrawn or scaled back. Such initiatives, if they have been produced from scratch and are bespoke to the organization, can be very costly and show limited ROI (return on investment) if they change every two or three years. The trend towards employees spending less time with each employer in a typical 40-year career simply leads to having to do more 'company-wide programmes' than ever before with diminishing returns. The mobility of key executives in HR and marketing also affects this return as new programme sponsors every two or three years means more 'new' programmes for long-term employees to go through to reflect the latest industry thinking about what could work only slightly better. Employees often perceive new HR or internal comms initiatives as 'the next new thing' unless they are deeply rooted in the values of the organization.

It also has to be said that, with the rise of social networking and communication outside the confines of work, the current crop of 20- and 30-year-olds are much less compliant as employees than previous generations were. Organizations should be mindful that paying attention to internal corporate communication comes a long way down the must-do list when employees are constantly on social networks and liaising with colleagues during their working day. Many junior and middle-level employees have more than one personal communications device with them at any one time in addition to what the organization provides. This is yet another example of media fragmentation and a diminishment of the 'voice' of the employer. Engagement with employees therefore needs to be earned; it is no longer a right which employers can expect to exercise just because they happen to pay employees a salary every month.

Building the case for engagement

Let's tackle the fundamental issue: why bother to introduce an engagement initiative at all? You always need clear, well-researched business reasons for introducing new initiatives into any organization. In marketing, you are unlikely to persuade the senior stakeholders to invest in a change in your advertising proposition unless you are pretty sure it is going to work – it costs money and no one wants to see it wasted. In HR, changing remuneration policy could have wide-ranging consequences for many years, both financial and legal. So presenting a revised engagement policy is not going to be successful unless the research has been conducted professionally. Changing the way you intend to encourage stakeholders to connect with your brand needs a strong organizational rationale or it simply won't get done.

So the first question to ask in your quest for strategic brand engagement is quite simply, will it work and will it deliver better financial returns than not doing it at all? Marks & Spencer, the UK retailer, devotes a number of pages of its regular employee survey to factors related to engagement. When all the numbers are in, the rates and results analysed and the moderations completed, those stores with the highest and lowest scores on engagement correlate closely to those with the highest and lowest sales per square foot of retail space.

Employee engagement

The good news is that a number of reputable consultancies and global brands have been keeping records of the financial and psychological effects of brand engagement since the early 1990s. There are four or five important studies that constantly crop up when talking about employee engagement on a global basis. It is well worth knowing about them and being able to get more detail about them if someone questions the facts behind what you are advocating:

- In its review of engagement initiatives implemented during the previous decade, a *Harvard Business Review* in 2000 concluded: 'Research has clearly and consistently proved the direct link between employee engagement, customer satisfaction and revenue growth.' A typical study from this period was a Stanford Business School report by Hannan and Baron in 1996 that looked at Silicon Valley start-ups. It concluded that those organizations that implemented various types of employee 'commitment' models, such as family-type working environments of trust and pastoral care, were most likely to go public more quickly and had a higher likelihood of survival than those that were more autocratic in style.

- In 2005 Towers Perrin, the management consultancy, gathered opinions from 85,000 people across 16 countries over four continents about 'employee performance potential'. It concluded that 'highly engaged workers' can and often do contribute more to an enterprise or organization and its financial results than those who are not engaged. It recorded that 84 per cent of highly engaged employees believed they can make a positive impact to the quality of their products compared with only 31 per cent of the disengaged employees. In the same report 72 per cent of the engaged group said they could positively improve customer service compared with 27 per cent of the disengaged group. Sixty-eight per cent said they could see ways to cut costs within their organization's processes whereas only 19 per cent of the disengaged thought they could. There is a clear message here about identifying highly engaged employees and enrolling them in schemes to contribute to the more efficient running of the enterprise.

- In 2008 IBM partnered with the Human Capital Institute to examine the financial track records of 287 publicly-quoted US organizations and the link, if any, with employee engagement measures. They found that those organizations that were focused on 'measuring and addressing employee engagement', aligning them with organizational goals, outperformed those who did not have programmes to address these topics.

- The following year, 2009, Gallup showed that engaged employees are more profitable, customer-focused and loyal than disengaged employees.

- Since 1998 Great Place to Work surveys, undertaken by the GPTW Institute, San Francisco, have consistently shown that there is a direct correlation between a US organization's position in the GPTW Top 100 list and the Standard & Poor's top 500 enterprises.

- Costco US is an easy-to-understand and compelling example of how engagement can make a difference, especially in their retailer environment of wafer-thin margins. In the mid-2000s it was recording 23 per cent employee turnover vs an industry average of 66 per cent and higher per head productivity than any comparable retailer at the time. This followed a deliberate campaign of new investment in employee benefits, extensive employee skills training and a number of policies designed to instil a high degree of trust between the managers and the managed. This could be a classic definition of how to engage with employees.

It is clear from all these studies that almost regardless of the economic cycle or the sector you work in it makes financial sense to run employee engagement activities. Those who do are likely to survive longer, improve their sales and have higher employee retention than direct competitors, which by definition means lower core operating costs and better customer service. There is always an argument to be made that other factors were in play such as a new product launch or a revitalized advertising proposition. But the more engagement case histories you collect the better both the circumstantial and the actual evidence looks.

So far, so good. But isn't it obvious that if you treat employees well, ask for their opinions and involve them in internal improvement processes, you will get a better result? It feels right as an idea but does it really deliver substantial bottom-line profits? After all, there are substantial costs associated with professional and consistent internal marketing. Here are some case studies which the C-suite needs to know about: Sears, the US retailer; John Lewis, the UK retailer; LV=, the UK insurer and The Gallup Organization.

CASE STUDIES

Sears: Measuring the ROI of engagement

Following the global recession in the 1990s most retailers across the developed world downsized to avoid going out of business. Sears, the US retailer, took a counter-intuitive route. It maintained its employee levels and invested in engagement strategies instead. The argument went that analyzing employee engagement, measuring it and playing it back to employees would lead to better customer retention, more sales, better employee retention, lower costs and higher profits. And so it proved. A *Harvard Business Review* report about Sears spanning the early 1990s period stated:

> By enabling employees to see the implications of their actions it changed the way everyone at Sears thought and acted. The bottom line reflected this changed behaviour: the merchandise group went from a loss of nearly $3 billion to a net income of $752 million in 1993.

The key point was that Sears discovered for itself that it could actually correlate a specific increase in 'engagement score' with actual sales revenue. It discovered that an increase in five points for engagement for any manager's team always resulted in half of one per cent increase in sales revenue growth from that team. It does not sound instantly impressive. But if you consider that those who undertake engagement activities for the first time often increase their levels of engagement by as much as 10 percentage points then the revenue improvements could be enormous, all other things being equal.

John Lewis Partnership, UK

The John Lewis Partnership (JLP) in the UK was one of the pioneers of 'mutual' employment, establishing itself before World War I. Its 81,000 employees are known as 'partners' – they co-own the business and have done so since 1950. For over 10 years JLP has been running monthly employee surveys which cover a wide range of internal management topics and have developed the technique into a key tool for two-way dialogue within the organization.

The values of the organization are to promote the 'happiness' of partners, to build a sustainable business long term, to serve customers to the best of each person's abilities and to show care with regard to the local community and the environment in general. Policies and internal processes have been developed over the years to support these principles of operational activity. All employees receive the same percentage of salary bonus, which can go up or down, depending on annual corporate profits. They are 'all in it together' on relatively equal terms, so all employees have a vested and strategic reason to act out the shared values whenever they get an opportunity. All employees are fully aware of those shared values and they drive every aspect of their delivery of customer service.

It seems to work. During the first half of 2012 JLP recorded a 60 per cent increase in profits against a backdrop of a static Western economy and a UK and Eurozone recession. Partners celebrated with bonuses, even after implementing a 'price promise' to match prices for specific, branded items sold by its competitors. The bonus was equivalent to 14 per cent of salary from a sales increase, year on year, of 6 per cent.

LV= increased engagement and the results followed

Case histories of engagement success do not always have to be about well-known names. Take LV= in the UK, for example, which employs around 4,000 people and sells car insurance, amongst other products. Liverpool Victoria, the original organization, was founded in 1843 – a long-established but somewhat conservative insurance company. It was losing ground against some of the more aggressively marketed domestic insurance competitors. Although the Group could demonstrate substantial underlying profits, in 2006 the General Insurance (GI) division recorded a loss of £22 million. Something had to be done.

A new senior management team was appointed and quickly concluded that the most critical issue was the ongoing loss of 10,000 customers a month due, partly, to poor customer service. At the time researchers discovered that there was a pervasive culture of 'jobs for life' and that performance did not really matter. Newly-appointed Head of Engagement, Karen Sharpe, commented:

> The culture was undynamic, matriarchal and old-fashioned: the message was 'we'll care for you no matter how good or bad you are at your job'. So people were not using their initiative, they were just doing the bare minimum and were not 'involved' in what they were doing.

The prevailing management style was for decision-makers to stay in their ivory towers and remain somewhat aloof from their team members. Customer Service Representatives worked in an atmosphere of hierarchical fear; there were no organization-wide agreed procedures for dealing with customer queries and no recognition for exceptional performance or assessing customer service performance.

LV= embarked on a six-year programme of engagement initiatives based on a complete re-engineering of the culture and internal processes. Engagement, as measured through an employee survey, rose from 64 per cent in 2007 to a high of 83 per cent in 2011, against an industry average score of 71 per cent. What was more important were the financial results. The number of motor insurance policies sold rose from 106,000 to 708,000. Profits improved with a rise of 327 per cent.

No one is suggesting it was all down to the engagement programme as the behaviour change of the management team and focus on key performance indicators clearly had significant parts to play. But the circumstantial evidence for tackling employee engagement is strong.

Gallup: Human Sigma research

A common cry from those who are unaware of the impact that engagement policies can have is: if it's that effective, can you prove it? This is precisely what Gallup, the management consultancy, attempted to do with its 'Human Sigma' initiative. In 2003 it revealed that, in a survey of 10 organizations across 1,979 separate business units, those who undertook to strengthen their employee–customer engagement activity outperformed their closest five peers by 26 per cent, when measured by gross margin.

Gallup developed its Q12 (12 questions) tool for measuring employee engagement, which is now arguably the most widely used engagement tool in the world. Used in conjunction with the CE11 (to measure customer engagement) the Human Sigma is a measure of engagement levels across a wide spectrum of organizational engagement activity. The main benefit is that it can be used to compare and contrast engagement levels between organizations so it becomes a sector and industry-wide benchmarking tool for engagement best practice as well as a local tool for specific intervention.

Six Sigma is the well-known quality tool that manufacturers have used for many years to assess and benchmark the quality of their processes. Human Sigma is an extension of this principle to achieve consistency of employee engagement by including customer engagement as a single measure. The measurements are based on a five-step system:

1 Measure and manage both employee and customer engagement together as an organic entity.

2 Measure feelings and emotions, not just facts.

3 Measure engagement locally and intervene locally.

4 Create a single measure, the Human Sigma.

5 Improvement comes from intervention in weak areas and at the local level.

The emphasis on feelings is well made. Gallup discovered a performance distinction between customers who are 'rationally engaged' and those who are 'emotionally engaged'. As all advertising people know, customers like to hear and learn the reasons to buy. But they actually commit to buy with their hearts and emotions, when push comes to shove, in a competitive trading environment. Human Sigma identifies employees and customers who are emotionally engaged and therefore more likely to be more loyal and spend more. John Fleming, Gallup, co-authored an article with Jim Aslund on Gallup's Human Sigma model, and they point out:

> In our own research we have observed that building a critical mass of engaged employees contributes significantly to the bottom line. In a recent study of 89 companies we found that the companies that build this critical mass of engagement have earnings per share (EPS) at 2.6 times the rate of companies who do not. (Fleming and Aslund, 2005)

The point about emotional engagement is that to be successful organizations need to build a critical mass of emotionally engaged employees *and* emotionally engaged customers to outperform their peers. It is not a predictive tool for success if only one side of the equation has been tackled.

So, what is this magic formula and why 'sigma'? In mathematics the Greek letter *sigma* represents standard deviation, in other words the distribution of items around a specific set of variables:

FIGURE 2.1   Gallup Human Sigma formula

$$HS = \sqrt{(EEpercentile \times CEpercentile)} \times \left(\frac{percentile\,Max}{percentile\,Min} \right)^{0.125}$$

According to Gallup's formula, Human Sigma is a single measure of employee engagement and customer engagement combined, represented as an overall score. So interpreting the formula in Figure 2.1, HS means the Human Sigma score for that particular work group. Provided both the employee score and the customer score is better than the average or mean (50 or more on a scale of 1–100) you then multiply them together and derive its square root. The resulting figure then needs to be adjusted to take into account the differential between the highest percentage score in the group and the lowest factored to the power of 0.125 – a statistical device to ensure that the score is as representative as possible when comparing it with other scores from other groups. If either of the two scores is below the median (below 50 on a scale of 1–100) then the calculation is as shown in Figure 2.2.

FIGURE 2.2   Gallup Human Sigma sub-median formula

$$HS = \sqrt{\frac{(EEpercentile \times CEpercentile)}{2}}$$

For the purposes of comparison with other groups being scored, the HS score can then be categorized into one of six levels, ranging from HS1 through to HS6. Broadly speaking an HS1 score is poor and an HS6 score is excellent.

The point about Human Sigma is that those groups scoring highly are more emotionally engaged with the organization, perform better when they interact with customers (produce repeat sales) and stay longer as employees. Various studies have shown that on average only 20 per cent or so of employees could be said to be highly engaged, so there is plenty of scope to make interventions to improve this average score.

More engagement dividends

It is always useful to have available some undeniable statistics to show the potential effectiveness of any new management technique. Here are just a few for employee engagement, taken from *Engaging for Success*, a UK Government report published in 2009:

- Engaged employees in the UK take just 2.69 sick days a year, compared with disengaged employees who take 6.19 days, on average;

- 87 per cent of engaged employees are less likely to leave their employment than those who are disengaged;

- 78 per cent of engaged employees would recommend their own organization's products to consumers whereas only 13 per cent of disengaged employees would.

Costs vs benefits

As with all organizational initiatives you can 'buy' organizational change if you put enough resources behind it. Sales incentives are a good case in point. If an enterprise wants to improve its market share through its channels, short-term incentives can and do produce substantial increases in sales revenue from anywhere between 10 and 50 per cent or more, depending on the market and the level of incentive offered. But such interventions cost money. So the question is, how do we calculate the ROI for engagement activities?

Many consultancies and enterprises have published case studies to show how they have justified the specific business case for undertaking employee engagement. Most are based on calculating the loss from disengaged employees (but not from disengaged channel partners... that is another story). CTS (The Center for Talent Solutions) found that over the years 'fully engaged' employees produce 20–25 per cent better performance than those who are neutral in terms of engagement; see Figure 2.3.

FIGURE 2.3 Financial impact of engagement

Financial Impact of Engagement
Will 'engagement talent' impact our financials?

		Estimated Organization Employee Base:	25,000		
		Corporate 'Weighted Average' Total Salary and Benefit Cost:	$89,750		
				CURRENT financial impact of employee engagement	
Engagement Level	Performance Delivered	Bottom Line Impact		% Organization	Financial Impact
LEVEL 4 Fully Engaged	125%	Organization GAINS $22,438 per year		10%	$56,093,750
LEVEL 3 Engaged	100%	Employee delivers an organization 'value' equal to the costs (salary + benefits)		65%	$NIL
LEVEL 2 Somewhat Engaged	75%	Organization LOSES $(22,438) per year		20%	$(112,187,500)
LEVEL 1 Disengaged	50%	Organization LOSES $(44,875) per year		5%	$(56,093,750)

Annual Impact of Engagement $(112,187,500)

What is the financial impact per share? 997,839,000 Shares   (0.11)

SOURCE: Human Capital Institute, Allan Schweyer, 2009

You can see from the figure that the high levels of disengagement caused a financial drag on the organization of some $112 million. By raising the number of those 'fully engaged' to 20 per cent the positive financial impact would be $56 million. Clearly this is a large enterprise of some 25,000 employees so the benefit numbers are also substantial. You would need to factor in the cost of any engagement strategies and activities. But in the context of over $50 million additional revenue, my guess is that the intervention cost for 25,000 employees would be less than $5 million, so somewhat small compared with the gain.

By any measure it is clear that there are revenue gains and ongoing cost savings to be made by engaging employees more directly in what they do at work. How they engage with customers also has a defined impact on an organization's market share and consumer loyalty.

The costs of disengagement

The opposite is also true. Organizations with high levels of disengagement suffer in many ways, so it is worth having arguments in place to counteract those who are inclined to do nothing. The costs of workplace frustration can be staggeringly high and yet according to the 2009 Accor *Reward to Engage* survey, 75 per cent of business leaders have no specific engagement strategy for employees. Barriers to implementing engagement strategies include:

- Inter-personal problems with direct line managers and supervisors.
- Lack of confidence in senior management.
- Non-provision of basic needs and benefits appropriate to the sector.
- Poor line communication, low incidence of public recognition.

All these can be remedied with the right strategic approach that covers the basic areas of deficiency.

Channel partner engagement

But what about channel partners? In the same way that barriers to successful interaction or engagement with employees and customers can be broken down and eliminated by sound engagement activities, channel partner barriers can be eliminated or at the very least lowered. A series of interventions such as eliminating concern that the organization will buy direct from wholesalers or other similar partners, respecting geographical territories, participating in post-sale activities, investing in training and education, choosing partners through which customers prefer to buy, devizing recognition schemes... all these activities will improve the percentage of 'fully engaged' channel staff. This will have a bottom-line impact that goes beyond the normal return you might expect from sales incentives or similar promotional activity.

So, to answer the question about why engagement matters, we can summarize the response across several areas. Organizations with high rates of employee engagement show more than double the growth rate of those who do not. Highly emotionally-engaged customers buy more product than those who buy rationally. The jury is still out on the behaviour of channel partners. But logic tells us that engaging channel partner staff using similar engagement techniques to those the organization uses for employees must result in more interaction with their end customers about the organization's products rather than someone else's. The question is how much channel intervention is required and at what cost, beyond the purely financial arrangement of distribution deals and discounts for volume.

We have explored what strategic brand engagement is and why it matters to any size of organization. The next question to consider is how to get started and what sort of intervention to undertake. To get there, we need first to understand what your brand is and what job it does for you, your customers, your employees and your channel partners.

What is a brand?

03

> *A brand is a gut feeling about a product, service or company.*
> *It's not what you say it is. It's what they say it is.*
>
> **(MARTY NEUMEIER, NEUTRON LLC)**

In the opening chapter we touched on the idea that a brand is not just the logo or emblem of an organization. The brand is an expression of all the thoughts and ideas that surround the organization, which is shared between employees, customers, channel partners and the wider world in varying and unequal amounts. A brand often changes over time although brand owners would like to think it is constant. A brand image has a financial value in many markets: by supporting the brand you are also supporting a valuable organizational asset. A good brand encourages people to buy regularly and consistently and may well have been built up over decades and, in a few cases, centuries. But it can also be destroyed over a weekend if it is not managed as carefully as any physical or financial asset. A good brand offers a promise to consumers that if they buy the product or service it will deliver on that brand promise.

A brand does not necessarily need to be a tangible product. In fact in large parts of the Western economy brands are increasingly based on service and know-how or knowledge rather than things that are manufactured in factories. An organization with a positive brand image can 'extend' its brand way beyond the core skills of the original organization, although remaining in a perceived, related area of expertise. Caterpillar is a $20 billion US construction plant company, but it also sells 'Cat' branded boots and outdoor clothing of all kinds. This activity only represents 5 per cent of its entire revenue. But still, 5 per cent of $20 billion is a substantial contribution to the organization's financial health.

A brand can also extend into seemingly unrelated business sectors. Virgin Records begat Virgin Airlines and eventually financial services, wedding planning and railways, amongst other businesses. The only consistency appears to be the founder and owner Sir Richard Branson who inspires such trust and credibility that Virgin customers are likely to buy anything from one of his organizations because the brand represents a certain level of quality and style.

Trust is the key essence of any brand. The organization does not necessarily have to be known for creating a particular type of product, but it does need to be trusted to be able to deliver and stay in business for the long term. As Wally Olins, the British design and branding expert says: 'Overall, because branding is about creating and sustaining trust it means delivering on promises. The best and most successful brands are completely coherent. Every aspect of what they do and what they are reinforces everything else' (2007).

Rebuilding trust

Most large organizations now take the issue of consumer trust and confidence in their products very seriously. Often the bigger an organization is, the more it has to lose. This was not always true in earlier times. In fact many of the world's biggest brands have a somewhat chequered history when it comes to humility in the face of a changing market. IBM's now famous statement supporting its business strategy of continuing to concentrate on providing computers for business rather than the mass market – 'Who the hell needs a computer in their home?' – is as ludicrous-sounding now as it was arrogant then. In these days of instant communication reputations built up over decades can be lost in weeks, unless the organization understands brand engagement.

CASE STUDY   Tesco

In Europe during February and March 2013 there was a scandal in the food industry chain. Following routine DNA testing of 'beef' in fast food products such as frozen burgers, horsemeat was found to be present in the meat mix, right across the supplier chain. There is nothing inherently wrong with horsemeat; in fact it is leaner than beef and arguably healthier. But the products did not carry any labelling to show that horsemeat was being used. As far as the consumer was concerned this deception – because horsemeat is much cheaper to produce than beef – was a serious breach of trust. One hundred per cent 'beef', as promoted on the packaging, turned out to be 80 per cent horsemeat.

Many major European supermarkets and retail grocery outlets removed the products in question from their shelves and consumers voted with their wallets by shunning beef products entirely. Tesco, the leading British supermarket, took the unprecedented step of running double-page high profile advertisements in all the daily newspapers to apologize for the error in service over a period of weeks, specifically admitting that its internal processes were 'part of the problem'.

It resolved to 'change the way we do things... to make things better.' At the same time it declared that it was no longer going to source certain meat and vegetable products mainly from overseas and would be supporting their indigenous suppliers, whenever possible. This change of buying policy hit a significant chord with UK food chain suppliers who had been complaining for many years that Tesco was not supporting its UK suppliers as much as it could. The advertisements ended with the sign-off: 'This is it. We are changing.'

Most market leaders who make a mistake simply say sorry and leave it at that. But in the Tesco example it is very clear that it saw the mistake as a potentially catastrophic breach of trust in its brand that had to be rectified immediately if it were to regain good perceptions of the brand and, of course, future profits. Quite simply, it could not afford, as a business, to do nothing and hope it would blow over and be forgotten. Engaging with suppliers and customers simultaneously in this unusual admission of fault and public reparation through changing its internal procurement process is a classic example of strategic brand engagement in practice. By making the connection between brand reputation with consumers and behaviour in the channel, Tesco already had a policy to deal with the issue, rather than having to debate whether they are or should be connected. This is joined-up brand management done well.

CASE STUDY   SSE

At around the same time SSE, a major UK utilities services provider, had just been fined by the UK Government for sharp sales practice in encouraging consumers to switch their utilities provider without supplying adequate financial comparisons. In the past most major players would have just kept quiet and taken the official fine on the chin as part of doing business. But SSE decided to formally 'apologize' to its consumers by taking full-page media advertisements with the headline: 'Sorry isn't enough.' It then went on to say that the way it sold energy to consumers in the past 'wasn't good enough', that it was changing the way it did business, and set up a compensation fund for those consumers who were affected. It finished the publicity by stating: 'We're not perfect, but we hope you can see how far we have come. And we'll keep working hard to make sure we don't make the same mistakes again.'

So branding is not just corporate identity or another name for what the marketing department does. For many businesses the brand is trust in the business – the real reason why employees are loyal, why channel partners want to partner and why customers continue to buy from you, even in the face of the toughest competition on price or value for money.

Where did brands come from?

The practice of putting a recognizable mark on something you own is as ancient as human society itself. In pre-literate times you did not have to know how to read to see which animals belonged to which farmer: a distinctive mark on each animal was enough. The Romans were probably the first to exploit internationally the wider application of a brand through its use of the SPQR *(Senatus Populusque Romani)* slogan, which they placed on military insignia as well as on coins. It was a sign of power and support throughout their empire and suggested that anything or anyone carrying items with this symbol was part of a much wider organization that could be relied on to support the bearer. It was not only a guarantee of value but a promise that the sponsoring organization could be relied upon to follow through. Later, armed forces, the Church and landowners copied this idea so that in times of conflict or dispute people who could not read knew who they were dealing with… and sometimes who to complain to.

Marks of quality

It was not until the late post-industrial revolution age that commercial enterprises began to see the attractions of adding an owner's mark to goods. The first types of product to get the branding treatment were pharmaceutical pills and potions. Poor environmental conditions and a lack of medical infrastructure in many big cities led to the large-scale manufacture and distribution of all kinds of medicines and palliatives to ease the symptoms of bad digestion, viruses and general ill-health caused by industrialization and people living together at close quarters.

Their growth was fuelled by the first mass market newspapers and a population, at least in the West, who could read, in the main. The manufacturer's name was shown prominently so that consumers could ask for the product by name. Later on, to distinguish similar products from each other, extravagant claims were made for a particular product with memorable, catchy slogans. Coca-Cola started life as a headache remedy and general medical pick-me-up before becoming simply a drink. The main point about early branding was that the manufacturer's name was a sign of consistent quality and that you could rely on the product being effective or of a known quality as long as it carried that particular manufacturer's name.

Products needed to be differentiated

In the second half of the 19th century it was clear to manufacturers that new industrial technologies made it possible to produce large numbers of personal items at ever lower prices and that ordinary people now had enough spare money at the end of the week to spend discretionally on such products.

But it was not enough to simply design their own posters or write their own advertisements in local newspapers and hope for the best. They could see that there was a skill involved in both writing the advertisements and negotiating with the media owners. The movement towards using an 'agent' to do it for you was where modern advertising and marketing agencies originated. This was the pioneering age of the publicity agent who provided the design and writing skills for 'free' in return for a cut in the media spend. Although the advertising industry no longer works in this way, it was common right up until the mid-1970s for large advertising agencies to make most of their revenue from media commissions rather than creative, consultancy and other promotional work.

Poster advertising for tea, chocolate and soap represented the golden age of mass advertising and provided the opportunity for product owners to create memorable and lasting images at the point of purchase through posters and, later on, newspapers. The Pears soap advertisements of the 1880s, featuring Sir John Millais's now famous 'Bubbles' image, are a good example of owner-driven advertising but with the twist of a big idea such as a memorable image. This represents the first steps in modern branding where the product people buy is not simply what the product does for you. It includes a range of intangible impressions and feelings of affinity with the overall brand promise.

CASE STUDY   Lever's Pure Honey

During the 1870s something curious had been happening to the seemingly simple task of using the manufacturer's name to attract sales. William Lever, son of a grocer from Lancashire, UK, had noticed the consumer demand for butter and eggs. He thought that perhaps soap might also be a discretional product the new city dwellers might buy, as many worked in filthy conditions with no obvious, alternative product to clean themselves with after work. Soap was then currently available as a grey, anonymous slab, cut into manageable pieces by the producers on demand. He decided to call it 'Lever's Pure Honey' rather than just Lever's soap so that it would be memorable. It was. So much so that other entrepreneurs quickly copied his 'honey' idea. He responded by not only creating another soap with a name as before, 'Sunlight', but added a box with instructions on how to use it. This was later followed by 'Lifebuoy', which played upon its disinfectant quality and again was sold in a box with instructions. 'Guard Your Children from City Contagions' ran one famous headline in 1923.

It is clear from these early days of mass product promotion that enhancing simple commodity products was an effective way of differentiating your goods from competitors' offerings. The additional cost of an instruction booklet, a box or other special packaging made it easier for consumers to make a choice, not just one based on price.

Unilever, and its great rivals Procter & Gamble in the United States, went on to create world-famous products but all with a starting point that promotion and packaging were as important and sometimes more important than the product itself, in terms of the time and effort taken to differentiate it from their competitors. By the 1950s commodity products such as breakfast cereal, coffee, beans, toiletries, etc, known as FMCG (fast moving consumer goods), were largely created by brand managers who concentrated on market research and promotion rather than the manufacture of the product itself. The reason was purely commercial. Simple products could be turned out by almost any manufacturer. The key to success was how that product differed from its equally effective competitors in the market and, to a lesser extent, how it was distributed at the retail level. Resources and intellectual effort were aimed at delivering what the consumers say they want and in a way that the channel says they can sell it to them better.

So, the FMCG brand is a carefully considered amalgam of all this research, distributor preference and price points wrapped up in as simple a promotional proposition as possible. It is clear then that a brand is not just the product being sold.

The rise of service businesses

That's all very well for a relatively simple commodity product like soap. But what about services? Of course service businesses have been around for much longer than commodity businesses. Long before the invention of coins and money in general, people have traded services with each other simply to survive. The farmer paid his workers in crops; hunters shared the meat they had with the spear-maker; mothers cooked what the fathers caught in the wild. Exchanging services was the way vast swathes of society worked until monetary systems, industrialization, automation and the migration into cities meant services could be delivered for money, which in turn could be used later for goods.

Most books about marketing and HR tend to use industrial and product examples to make their points. But as we move into the 21st century a more appropriate model would be service businesses. Not only do most Western economy employees work in services, most of what we buy is now service-oriented, even if it looks like you have bought a product. In terms of branding we need to understand why a service is different from a commodity. For a start it is much more to do with the people element of overall product delivery. As soon as you involve people as an integral part of the brand promise, you have a problem. Because at some stage you will need to engage the sellers and the employees in the delivery of the product, but because they are human the quality of delivery is variable and inconsistent.

The early days

Most people in Western economies are no longer working to survive. Although it may sometimes feel that you have no income to speak of left over at the end of the month, it is normal for employees (who are also consumers) in the 21st century to have somewhere to live, running water, a source of electricity, basic furniture and enough to eat. In Europe more adults have cell phones than do not, if you count how many phones are currently in use. If people don't have jobs the State provides a minimum income to prevent large-scale destitution.

What's left after basic needs are met is discretional expenditure and the 21st century commercial model is built on the fact that there is a considerable opportunity to sell non-essential products and services in order to attract that discretional spend. A significant proportion of monthly consumer spend involves people doing things for other people. In primitive times a neighbour or relative would do this in exchange for another service. But in the post-industrial West services are delivered on a commercial basis, which means you have to pay for them. Often the services are very similar so consumers have a choice as to who to buy them from, subject to the usual constraints of price and location. And where there is a choice and variance of quality, there is branding.

CASE STUDY   Automotive – from manufacturing to branding

Selling cars is a good example of why branding is an important concept for non-marketers to understand, especially from the employee engagement viewpoint. In Henry Ford's day, you could have any Model T Ford car you wanted as long as it was black, so the saying goes. The uniqueness and desirability of the product meant that the manufacturer could call the shots and decide to a large extent what the consumer got. (Apple manages to do this with some of its unique products, causing hysterical queues whenever the 'must-have' new gizmo is released across the world.) For Ford this kept costs down and made manufacturing extremely efficient. It seems self-evident that if there was only one type of mass market car available then there was not much call for branding as we understand it today. Branding only arises when there is consumer choice and product owners need to differentiate their product from the direct competitor.

As more cars became available, advertising developed to differentiate the various models. As more cars competed within the same sector manufacturers then turned to their channel partners, in this case car showroom dealers, to provide that differentiation in terms of initial purchase, inclusive extras at point of sale and aftersales service. In essence buying a car meant buying into a long-term commitment to the people infrastructure that the dealer provided. In many instances manufacturing was often conducted at a loss in order to acquire and retain service contracts and that all-important second or replacement car. Choice of car is a personal issue for many consumers and attachment to a particular manufacturer is hard to break.

So the job of car advertising and wider branding is to reassure existing customers and their friends and relatives that they have bought the right product. Along the way they would hope to achieve some 'conquest' sales from completely new prospects. But in the main branding cars is about retaining existing customers and selling more through their friends and acquaintances. Car buyers loyal to one brand become brand ambassadors and largely do the selling work for the manufacturer, with dealers being available to 'take the order'.

Social networking through word of mouth, rather than digitally, has always been there. The only difference today is that online networks mean the word gets round more quickly so manufacturers need to be much quicker on their feet if the brand is damaged by a recall or some other product quality issue.

The removal of international trade blocks, particularly within Europe, provided yet another stimulus for competition. Most industrial countries could boast of having an indigenous car industry from the 1950s through to the 1980s as they not only provided skilled jobs locally but promoted general economic development through improved national mobility. But once barriers to international trade were removed, competition became global... and so did the branding.

The point about engagement in the automotive industry is that within the service chain that includes the product, the dealer, the service employees and the accessories suppliers there are multiple opportunities for disappointing the consumer. If the advertising does not truly reflect the product, then new owners will experience 'cognitive dissonance' – a perception that they have been sold a lemon – and will tell at least 10 other people, so researchers tell us, of their dissatisfaction. If the employees in the local dealership behave at odds with the brand expectations of consumers, they may think again about purchasing that type of car the next time around, even though rationally it suits their circumstances and their lifestyle. If the service employees do not provide a level of aftercare that customers have been led to expect with that particular car, they may not buy again when the time comes to replace it. These are all people and process issues that have nothing to do with the effective performance of the car or its engineering but are the basis on which the manufacturer has a long-term business or not... the brand.

'Me-too' products need more engagement support

In recent years there has been large-scale deregulation of utilities and other state-owned enterprises. As we have already learnt, if there is no choice or the product is unique there's no point in branding it because the product has a largely fixed market. Pre-deregulation, if you wanted electricity you bought it from the electricity company that supplied it to your area, but once competition was introduced there was a need to differentiate one supplier from another.

The first differentiation in utilities is clearly the price. Tariffs become an important differential, provided the consumer understands them. In the UK during 2013 the Government stepped back into the utilities market to rule that there should be no more than four tariffs, such was the diversity of offers marketed by utilities in a deliberate ploy to encourage inertia. It was argued, quite rightly, that consumers no longer had a choice because the differences were so bewildering that they stayed where they were rather than trying to fathom what the best deal around was.

Once price differentials are made clear, suppliers need to look for other differentiators. The most obvious differential is 'service'. In the case of utilities this means clear and prompt billing, uninterrupted supply of power and reliable engineers to fix any supply problems down the line. If a utility is going to claim that it is 'the simple alternative' to other competitors then its employees and sales people need to be telling the same story or consumers will go elsewhere... because now they can. This is a strategic brand engagement issue which the utilities industry is only just getting to grips with.

Telecoms branding

Another obvious example of a deregulated utility in search of branding is the telecoms industry. Once a monopoly service, the choice of telephone products has grown exponentially within the industrialized West and beyond. But as we all know the product being offered is no longer just the facility to speak to someone else at a time of our choosing in our home or office.

Handset, wireless technology has provided the technical basis for product differentiation. Initially we had a choice of voice and text; now with smartphones we have a myriad of facilities which draw on all the benefits of the internet while being on the move. More recently tablets have blurred the distinction between what is a telephone and what is a screen. The mini iPad is just one example of a convergence of products in the never-ending quest to be unique in a marketplace.

CASE STUDY   Apple and Samsung

The branding question here is how to encourage the consumer to buy a Samsung or an Apple product, and why? Samsung has a vast range of me-too electronic products with a strategy of continuing to add to that range so that consumers will move from TV to handset to washing machine, knowing that the quality promise of the Samsung brand will follow. Apple has a very small product range but they are all unique, well-designed, innovative products. Apple's strategy is to lead the market then move on to new innovations, taking its loyal customers with it and adding more as they go... the Virgin concept?

In both of these examples it is clear that there is a difference in how you deal with the service and people aspects of the product promise. Samsung uses the channel to distribute and service its products. Apple uses its own stores and engineers. Whether one way is better than another is not the issue. The key point is how each organization goes about engaging directly with its customers in terms of delivering the quality promise. More important is the question of whether the branding is carried through to all parts of the channel chain to reflect consistency, which in turn engenders loyalty and repeat purchase. Apple clearly thinks that it has to keep the selling aspects under close control so as not to compromise the brand promise. Samsung feels that the selling part can be outsourced without too much detriment to the brand promise. But someone somewhere needs to tell the employees and the channel what the values are and how to behave with loyal customers, for example.

Trust is easily lost

Brand loyalty can easily be lost if what you thought were the ethics and behaviour of the brand are found to be false. There is a famous marketing story in the UK of the Ratner jewellery chain whose CEO and co-founder Gerald Ratner described his products for the mass market as 'crap' in a business seminar to the trade in 1991. What he meant was that, compared with expensive, designer rings and necklaces, Ratner's products were not in the same category of desirability or value. The national daily newspapers carried the story, Ratner left the business and it had to be renamed, having been deserted by its, until then, loyal consumers. It was a sound business with £1 billion of sales revenue. But £500 million was wiped off its share price as a result of the episode. Trust in the Ratner name, rather than the business itself, had disappeared overnight and so the brand had to change.

The financial services brand

When Greg Smith resigned from Goldman Sachs at the height of the US financial crisis, he wrote in his resignation letter about 'the toxic and destructive culture' that investment bankers work in every day. There could not have been a better endorsement of the importance of the internal brand and how it translates directly into financial losses if you get it badly wrong.

Hewett and Arshad from Interbrand commented in *Argent*, the journal of a UK trade networking group called the Financial Services Forum, about the ongoing lack of trust in any consumer financial brand, not just the big brands:

> With the recession hitting the economies of Europe, banks have borne the brunt of the community's hardships and outbursts. But these same people are looking for banks that can demonstrate they are there to listen and learn, not tell and sell.
>
> (Hewett and Arshad, 2013)

They then outlined specific guidance on what banks should be doing to repair their brands:

- *Prove you want to lead the change.* For many months following the collapse of a number of formerly 'trusted' organizations, there was little or no communication to employees or the consumer about what banks were now doing to fix the problem.

- *Be clear about what you do.* In the past financial services institutions have played on the general lack of interest in the technical side of products and have muddied the waters about how much of the consumers' investment is actually being invested and how much is being taken in profit or commissions.

- *Care more about the way you work on the inside.* With the ever-invasive force of both public and private social networking media the inner management of the brand in terms of employee behaviour and processes can no longer go unexamined. If there is dubious practice internally, it needs to be challenged and dealt with before the consumer does it for you.

CASE STUDY   Tax and public trust

Throughout the first decade of the 21st century the Apple brand could do no wrong. Its products were innovative and distinctive. It seemed to hit the nail on the head when it came to relevance and performance, particularly with the 20–30-year-olds who had discretional money to spend on entertainment and social communication. In January 2013 Apple slipped from being the world's most valuable brand for the first time in many years. At around the same time it came to light that some $11 billion of its profits had been sheltered in various tax havens around the world. At the time a profitable corporation in the United States would expect to pay 35 per cent in corporation tax; Apple was only paying around 2 per cent. In the UK declared sales revenue was £1 billion but it only paid £14.4 million in tax to the authorities, an effective tax rate of just 1.44 per cent. This type of tax avoidance is not acceptable corporate behaviour on either side of the Atlantic when governments are running out of funds to pay for services in flat-lining economies.

Starbucks had to deal with a similar issue of trust after it came to light in 2012 that it paid virtually no tax on its European profits. After a public outcry and some local protests by consumers it decided to volunteer a fixed amount to the tax authorities in each country where no tax on profits was paid.

In the pre-Enron/Goldman Sachs/global banking crisis days it was thought 'clever' to avoid tax. But since the global downturn and the criminal proceedings for inappropriate behaviour by big businesses consumer opinion has shifted towards more openness and honesty. It appears consumers will no longer turn a blind eye to tax avoidance and brands can be severely damaged by not being sensitive to this new wave of sentiment. It remains to be seen whether Apple will have to modify its financial arrangements to keep the trust of its core consumers and therefore maintain its standing as a brand *par excellence*.

The chicken maharaja mix

The final piece in the branding jigsaw is what to do when you get very big. If your factory is on the same site as your HR and marketing departments, it is relatively straightforward to ensure employees and promotional agents are fully up to date with the organization's brand at all times. It is less easy to police the independent channel, but it can be done. Service companies have a more difficult issue in that standards of service (quality) have to be learnt and the outcomes monitored on a regular basis to maintain a consistent brand.

The solution to branding being delivered across many sites is to produce a set of rules or 'branding guidelines'. Outwardly this is a reference book of design templates that can be used to produce promotional messages when it is impractical to refer everything back to the centre. It becomes commercially impractical to do this internationally when foreign languages are involved and in some cultures certain colours or words suggest meanings not originally intended. One way around this is to create a 'master brand' so that at least the essence of the brand is carried accurately and applied appropriately wherever possible. This helps to get product recognition when you are using a range of promotional media to get your messages across.

McDonalds sells burgers internationally, sometimes as franchise operations and sometimes as wholly or partly-owned subsidiaries. In India the chicken burger product becomes a chicken maharaja mac, but the use of colour, logos and package design is standard across the world. Some brand marketers call this 'glocalization'. When franchises are granted, payments are often made for compliance with the branding rules and withheld if violated. The reason is a simple one: the organization has spent and continues to spend vast sums of marketing money promoting the product to be a recognizable sign of quality – a product consumers can trust. If the packaging and promotion do not match the quality promise then consumers will try another, probably cheaper product leading to loss of revenue. Consistent branding is a sign to the consumer of reliable quality.

Getting it right is not easy. Interbrand's *Best Global Brands 2012* report stated:

> Companies are competing aggressively not only against each other but also with local brands in countries such as China, Brazil, India, Bangladesh, Pakistan and Sri Lanka... agile and effective innovation among local competition has proven to be a critical factor that Unilever and PG have had to face around the world.

The answer is not simply to try and outspend local rivals in promotion but to work with the local channel to get products accepted as part of the commercial landscape through community deals and engagement projects. But in the final analysis consistency of quality is what emerging consumers seek and if the global brand can continue to deliver consumer satisfaction then locals will need to work hard to replicate in a few years what Western brand specialists have been doing successfully for decades.

Branding and long-term engagement

A final word of caution on inventing or re-inventing a brand. The qualities and attributes of any brand come from the perceptions of your products and organization by the consumers over long periods of time. These perceptions may go back decades in some circumstances.

CASE STUDY   British Airways

One of the most famous examples of this is when national UK carrier British Airways decided to change its aircraft livery. Traditionally, national airlines carry the national flag somewhere on the aircraft, or at least allude to it in design or typography. In 1997 BA (British Airways) launched its 'Utopia' re-brand, which used ethnic designs from around the world on the tailfins without a Union Jack in sight. The design, created by the Newell & Sorrel agency, was widely criticized in the media for abandoning the national flag. Even Prime Minister Thatcher famously covered the tail of a scale model with her handkerchief whilst on a trade visit, saying: 'We fly the British flag, not these awful things.' Two years later the repainting scheme was halted in favour of the tailfin design of then flagship product Concorde, reincorporating the British flag. The branding reversal was completed in 2011 when the original 1997 strapline, 'To fly. To serve' was fully reinstated.

It is virtually impossible to impose a brand on a market if there is a mismatch between what you say it is and what the market perceives it to be, unless you take rigorous action to overturn it. If you want to sell good (but not best quality) products to the mass market you need to promote them sincerely so that it reflects consumers' expectations. If they can trust you to tell the truth and they get what they expected, at an acceptable price, they will buy again. If you claim it is top quality, leading edge, multi-faceted and it isn't, watch the consumers vote with their cash and buy someone else's products next time.

There are some good examples in many markets of poorly perceived products turning themselves around. Certainly Tesco, the UK retailer, and Skoda, the state-owned Czech car manufacturer, were watchwords for poor quality and staff who did not care as much as they should in the 1970s. They have since turned their perceptions around, but not just by saying so with promotional statements. Both organizations re-engineered themselves from within with a new ethic of quality which just did not exist in their previous incarnations. This could not have been achieved without the substantial engagement of their employees and channel partners.

CASE STUDY   Pepsi vs Coke

The story of Coke's attempt to change its formula is well-documented. You mess with the brand at your peril. But a less well-known story is the one about whether Pepsi or Coke intrinsically tastes better or does the branding play any part in its appeal? The Baylor College of Medicine conducted a series of blind taste tests in 2004, pitching branded Pepsi and branded Coke against unbranded Pepsi and unbranded Coke and even against their own unbranded samples. In the unbranded versions both drinks proved equally popular with no discernible difference between the two. They then tried it again pitching Pepsi against an unbranded Coke. Pepsi drew. But when they tried branded Coke against unbranded Pepsi, Coke won hands down. Branded Coke even won handsomely against its unbranded self. The researchers concluded that 'Brand knowledge had a dramatic effect on subjects' behavioural preference' – so, nothing to do with the actual taste. As rational human beings we would like to dismiss consumer branding as 'just packaging' but there is something more fundamental going on here that is to do with historical engagement with the brand, not just the product's ingredients.

So what comes first, branding or engagement? If you already have a well-perceived brand, good for you. The task of improving brand engagement should be a useful way to highlight areas for improvement internally. Superior brands constantly question their own position in the world and take nothing for granted, not even being a market leader. We all need refreshing from time to time. But it probably did not start out with a superior brand image; it probably took many years to perfect. So there's no room for complacency in brand engagement. David Ogilvy, the advertising expert and writer defined the brand-building task as follows, making the point that although the world and markets change constantly the core personality of the brand remains: 'Build sharply defined personalities (or brand images) for your brands and stick to those personalities year after year. It is the total personality of a brand rather than any trivial product difference which decides its ultimate position in the market place' (Deye, 2012).

If you have no strong brand and would like to build one, you need to start the task with what consumers think of your organization and what your people think of you as managers. The next chapter deals with trying to define who you are as an organization and being specific about your uniqueness because this is what your engagement activity will be based on.

Who are you and who do you want to be?

04

> *We studied (visionary) companies in our research for* Built to Last: Successful habits of visionary companies *and found that they have outperformed the general stock market by a factor of 12 since 1925.* **(COLLINS AND PORRAS, 1996)**

Most organizations grow organically rather than start with a completely clean sheet. This creates a number of brand engagement problems. The successful founders and owners, with their undisputed authority, may no longer be part of the current management team. Typically those who found a business run things in a very different way to those who manage the business going forward. Employees also behave differently when the original founder leaves. New, acquiring owners are one step removed from the original driving idea and the ways of doing things on which the organization's ethos was based. Even with mature businesses, changes in technology or customer demographics may mean that a new approach may be needed more often than was expected in the past. Or perhaps a very strong competitor has emerged, either domestically or internationally, which has meant that doing things 'the same old way' is no longer as effective as it used to be. Difficult as it is to imagine, even Apple, one day, may lose its magic touch. When this happens, the brand changes too as does people's perceptions of it.

Cognitive dissonance

The reasons why many organizations find themselves not doing as well as they used to often lie in a mismatch between their brand (the accumulated assumptions of your values by employees, consumers and distributors) and how the brand's organization actually behaves towards consumers when they come into contact with it, typically during the after-sales process. Marketers call this phenomenon 'cognitive dissonance'. Consumers may know you as being good value for money but perhaps over the years your prices have crept up above the average for the products you sell. They may consider that you are innovative and leading edge – at least that's what your advertising still says – but you are running your business on out of date IT systems and your filing of data leaves much to be desired. Perhaps you consider yourself to be the expert in what you do, but there are so many competitors out there who are doing it more quickly and more efficiently than you that it's only a matter of time before customers begin to migrate to the more nimble providers. Employees may well know about this first because they are in constant touch with your market. But the senior team may well be in denial and would like to think it is just a question of changing parts of the process, cutting costs or doing more promotion. Consultants call this 'moving the deckchairs on the Titanic'.

Revaluation of all values

So there comes a time, eventually, when the senior team needs to take stock and 'pull up the drains', as they say. A discussion about vision and values is on the cards. But take care not to be seduced by quick fixes offered by operational experts who would like nothing better than to tinker with the engine or have some more resources to play with and then carry on as usual, rather than start all over again. Changing things is never comfortable:

- The first response to a decline in organizational performance is to cut costs. The reasoning is that the market is perceived as static or decreasing and that the only way to make more profits or maintain them at current levels is to reduce the overhead. This may well be a useful tactic in a temporary downturn. But if the market is actually slowly rising and your profits are not, it probably means you are being uncompetitive in some other way. Reducing the capacity to handle business will simply put pressure on the ability to deliver quality and even more customers will then turn to your competitors. So your action will actually accelerate the revenue decline rather than make it better.

- Another quick fix is to promote more. You can undoubtedly 'buy' additional sales through strong advertising to consumers and offering better incentives to the channel but this will only be for a short time. When the promotion stops, so will most of the new business in-flow. It may even fall back to lower levels than the pre-advertising period as consumers perceive you to have 'deserted the market'.

- A third option is to reduce your prices. Clearly many businesses do just this in static or declining markets. But there comes a point in the price curve where it begins to cost you more than you can gather in revenue to keep producing the same volume.

- Another tactic is to change the key executives. There may be genuine reasons why specific individuals may not be as effective as they used to be and they should be dealt with in the normal way. But it is unlikely that executives who have been successful for you for, say, the past 10 years have suddenly become useless.

- By far the most common technique is to change the person in charge overall. In theory this is not a bad idea as there is then an opportunity to look again at the overall plan and see if something obvious has been overlooked. However, if the new leader behaves just like the old one and uses a combination of the measures described above then nothing has really changed.

If you have tried all these options (tactics) and are still no further forward it is very likely that you need to take an uncompromising look at your overall plan (strategy) for the business to examine whether what you now offer the market is fundamentally different to when you were successful.

Vision and values

When retention rates of employees continue to fall, the channel is becoming harder and harder to get support from and consumers are spending with your direct competitors but not you, it represents a perfect storm in terms of the organization's place in the marketplace. It is a definition of general disengagement. It is time to revalue all your values and get to the bottom of what you are in business for and what type of organization is going to be successful in the current and future market.

There are some assumptions to make though. It goes without saying that, unless you are a very small business, you would hope to be operating in the same industry sector using the same or similar technology. It has to be assumed that you will use the same or similar plant and equipment. It is likely that you will be retaining most if not all of your employees. The key question is along the lines of 'What business are we in?' rather than 'What would we rather be doing?'

A common first reaction is to call a meeting of senior executives to 'discuss the problem'. It is likely that such discussions will have been had on a regular basis throughout the year as declining financial performance was analysed and blame was apportioned. Tactics to fix the problems as they come up will have been agreed and implemented, but to no avail. Having yet another meeting where fingers are pointed at various divisional or operational failures is not going to be productive. Regardless of what the numbers say, you need to examine the engagement levels of your various stakeholders to see if the problem lies in just one area or whether the entire organizational interface with the market is at fault.

Benchmarking

Benchmark your employee engagement

One way to start the process is to benchmark your level of employee engagement against a national or similar sector figure. That way you will be able to see whether your employees are as confused as you are as to why the organization is in decline.

We discussed in Chapter 2 how LV=, the UK insurance organization, improved its engagement score from 64 to 83 per cent. Clearly, to show an improvement down the line you have to have a base figure to start with. Whether you use a recognized international standard such as Gallup's Human Sigma 12-question survey or you devise your own, you need to start somewhere. The Gallup system gives you access to many thousands of organizations' results which means you can see whether you are above or below the average for your size and sector.

If you have never conducted an employee satisfaction survey before, you'll find that there are a number of proprietary employee satisfaction surveys marketed by consultants which reflect their own views about how to engage employees more effectively. Each one is slightly different and it depends whether you think the combination of questions would best reflect your current organizational thinking about what constitutes a 'good employee' or a 'good management style' within your sector.

Another way could be to invent your own employee survey and ask questions that follow the settled view of the main drivers for employee engagement. If you operate within the service sector you could use the results of the 2004 investigation by the Forum for People Performance Management and Measurement at Northwestern University, which looked at 100 US media organizations. The survey was split into three sections: organizational culture, organizational climate and HR systems. The research identified eight key drivers for what good employee satisfaction and engagement look like:

1 employee's intention to remain in the organization;
2 variety of skills employees can use;
3 level of customer service orientation;
4 degree of inter-unit coordination;
5 degree of job role conflict;
6 appropriate personal skills development;
7 level of autonomy;
8 respect for supervisor.

The principle is that if surveyed employees rated all these performance categories at 100 per cent they would be deemed to be 100 per cent satisfied and engaged in the enterprise. So the general question in each category would be: 'To what extent do you agree or disagree with the following statements...?' There will need to be some briefing notes before the survey goes ahead so that employees understand clearly what they are being asked.

These are all subjective views at any point in time, but the survey will produce an average number that the senior team can assess as being good or bad. For argument's sake let us assume that the overall score is 50 per cent, with the worst scores being 30 per cent for 'level of autonomy' and 'respect for supervisor'. This suggests that the workforce is somewhat lukewarm when it comes to feelings about the organization and that there is a significant problem when it comes to the employee/supervisor interface.

The individual, detailed verbatim comments will be useful as a guide to what vision and values to agree on. The aim would be to construct a set of values that improves the scores in each category, should you run the same survey 12 or 24 months later.

Benchmarking customer perceptions

There probably already exists a number of detailed marketing reports about product sales per market sector and where the organization's products lie in the competitor 'brand map'. There will be an ongoing promotional battle to position products in the optimum space to maximize sales revenues. But when it comes to strategic brand engagement we need to get a measure of what consumers think of their interactions with your employees. This is becoming even more important as products move online and the only human interface many potential consumers have with the brand is when they contact a calls management team or need to complain via e-mail or through independent feedback sites.

When it comes to values it is always useful to cross-check your consumers' perceptions of your products before having the 'vision' discussion. It is likely that your senior team is pretty clued-up on the current market position but it is worth re-circulating the brand marketing notes in case new joiners are not aware of any nuances or subtleties within certain markets of how your organization is perceived.

This type of research, though, is not about consumer positioning but more about human feelings when they interact with the organization's representatives. We are all familiar with the pre-recorded message that says that 'calls will be recorded and monitored' so that the organization can improve its customer service. Day-to-day feedback is necessary to improve skills development and check on individual performance but does little to help us understand how customers really feel about the organization.

The recommended route to finding out about deep-seated perceptions of your employees by customers is to hold focus, user or discussion groups. Usually, but not always, a representative sample of customers who have had recent interaction with employees will be mailed/e-mailed with a general survey asking them to rate employee performance across various process activities – making an initial enquiry, dealing with quotations, making an order, dealing with a complaint, for example, providing plenty of scope for verbatim comments in general about the organization's performance. Following this market sheep dip, small groups will then be invited to participate in a longer phone interview or a live discussion, conducted by a trained researcher, in a local hotel with say payment in retail vouchers or if appropriate discounts on your products. The results will provide a good comparison between how you think you are doing and how actual customers feel about the same touch points.

Benchmarking channel perceptions

The same principles apply to channel perceptions of your organization. In this case there will be an added element of the performance of your field employees who will be judged on how they portray your brand when they visit as part of their call cycle and how that perception differs from the 'master-brand' they experience as an end consumer. It may be for example that they know the brand very well as a consumer, including its perceived values and expectations of quality, only to be confused by the field team who may be projecting a completely different business ethic or way of doing things. If the consumer brand is all about quality but the wholesaler brand is about cutting corners and making do, you may have a problem.

Your brand in focus

There will be at least three strands to these reports, one for each engaged audience, which will contain numerous headlines. A trained researcher needs to pull them together as a short study for the senior team. Typically it will include:

- Current overall level of employee engagement with highlights of organizational values either being achieved or under-achieved.

- Perception of organizational values from customers who interact with employees at an individual level.

- Perception of the organization's values within the channel, whether that is your own employed sales team or independently-owned distributors.

The headline summary of such a report may read as follows:

The organization's master brand is a well-established, international premium provider of electronic goods. Its values are high quality products, reliable performance and being easy to deal with, as evidenced by its global and local advertising propositions. However the employees' survey shows that the perceived management style is highly risk-averse, does not welcome personal initiative and retention rates are lower than the industry average. The channel perceives the master brand to be at odds with their experience of dealing with the finance department in particular and other issues to do with product quality and returns.

CASE STUDY   Direct Line Group

In 2012 the Direct Line group, a UK insurance organization with 16,000 employees across 50 sites, was about to de-merge from the Royal Bank of Scotland and was concerned about the potential uncertainty this would create amongst employees. In particular the senior team wanted to redefine the culture and values so they could start the new business with true brand authenticity. After all, the new organization was no longer a top-down, rather paternalistic bank.

They decided to start by asking their employees across all silos of the enterprise what sort of organization they should be and asked them to suggest ethical and operational values which they felt they could deliver to their new and existing customers. This 'dialogue from the bottom up', as Paul Diggins, head of internal communications, called it, resulted in an employee training and communications programme called 'BEST'. Part of this organic process was to develop specific values for each of the operating divisions based on what is 'best' for the direct customer, whether internal or external.

Building the vision

You are now ready to have a serious discussion about what your brand actually is, what you would prefer your values to be rather than what they are actually perceived to be. But faced with the research you have gathered above, either formally or informally, you still have to put pen to paper and commit to something. There has been, and will continue to be, much discussion about what 'vision' means and how it differs from 'mission'. It does not matter a great deal what the technical definitions are, provided the senior team can agree what the difference is for their specific organization. It is worth getting this agreed early on to avoid confusion later when it comes to employee and channel briefings.

The vision, according to Collins and Porras (1996), is as good a description as any and worth using as a template:

> A well-conceived vision consists of two major components: core ideology and envisioned future. Core ideology, the yin in our scheme, defines what we stand for and why we exist... The envisioned future is what we aspire to become, to achieve, to create something that will require significant change and progress to attain.

The vision has an element of a future scenario about it and is distinguished from a mission statement by its aspirational aspects. The mission is a more detailed description of what your organization does now, your immediate goals and possibly your geographical spread. It follows on naturally as a specific statement of organizational intent from the vision. A good example is from the global energy management specialist Schneider Electric:

Vision: A world where we can all achieve more while using less of our common planet.

Mission: To help you make the most of your energy by providing innovative and efficient solutions and services to protect, power, cool and manage your critical systems.

You can see in this example that the vision is positive, idealistic and altruistic... all benefits to humanity in general. The mission is more organization-centric and details specific promises in terms of the commercial brand and what it delivers to customers.

Visions are usually more general and over-arching, as we will see later. Visions are at the heart of successful organizations; they can even be just the reason for the organization's existence. It is where the values come from and the eventual corporate plan itself. So it is useful to get the vision right from the very outset. Visions include your core ideology, your core values and some kind of envisioned future which should, if worded well, inspire everyone who comes into contact with the brand. As all marketing people know, finding the right words that everyone can agree with it not as easy as it sounds.

Core ideology

The first component of the vision, as stated above, is the core ideology of the organization, which would include the core purpose and the core values. For example, Google's stated vision is to 'organize the world's information and make it universally accessible and useful'. You can see in this description that the vision has no boundaries in the business of data management. But it is already moving into specific values, which are to be 'accessible and useful'. In terms of a driving force in the business, team leaders throughout the organization already have a steer from this broad statement that what they do going forward needs to match the stated criteria of accessibility and usefulness. Regardless of time, the economic cycle and the markets it works in, Google's vision remains the same.

So the core ideology is a fixed idea, a sense of purpose, an over riding aim, an enduring characteristic that is easy to communicate and simple to understand. Another example could be Hewlett Packard's core ideology, which is the 'dedication to affordable quality and reliability'. It remains a constant statement of what the organization is about, regardless of changes in the market or even the executive team that runs the business.

Core values

An organization's core values are statements of principle or beliefs that all employees can aspire to. They also form the basis of the brand to the outside world. They should cluster around the original vision, perhaps explaining in more practical terms how the vision can be supported and achieved. P&G (Procter and Gamble) formulated values based on a vision of product excellence. The Disney Corporation clusters its values around the core idea of 'imagination and wholesomeness'. Here are some examples of visions and values:

- *Anheuser-Busch.* Be the world's beer company. Through all of our products, services and relationships, we will add to life's enjoyment.
- *Caterpillar.* Be the global leader in customer value.
- *DuPont.* The vision of DuPont is to be the world's most dynamic science company, creating sustainable solutions essential to a better, safer and healthier life for people everywhere.
- *Heinz.* Our vision, quite simply, is to be the world's premier food company, offering nutritious, superior-tasting foods to people everywhere.

- *Kraft Foods (Mondelez)*. Our vision... Helping people around the world eat and live better.

Sometimes the vision needs more articulation before employees, consumers and distributors truly understand why this particular collection of phrases is a powerful differentiator – it needs to be unique, otherwise the brand will be perceived as 'another one of those kinds of organizations.' For example, Mazda Motors established a new corporate vision in December 1999, comprising three elements:

Vision: To create new value, excite and delight our customers through the best automotive products and services.

Mission: With passion, pride and speed, we actively communicate with our customers to deliver insightful automotive products and services that exceed their expectations.

Value: We value integrity, customer focus, creativity, and efficient and nimble actions and respect highly motivated people and team spirit. We positively support environmental matters, safety and society.
Guided by these values, we provide superior rewards to all people associated with Mazda.

Visions can be simple and concrete

But visions and values do not always have to be abstract concepts suitable for global market leaders. When Karen Sharpe and the engagement team at LV=, the UK insurer, began to tread down this new path, the articulation of the vision and values was remarkably straightforward. The key decision-makers and the senior team were already in the mutual insurance business and it had been a business since 1843. The vision, assuming it would stay as an insurance business, was to become one of the top five general insurers in the country using employee engagement and empowerment as the turnkeys for success. After much discussion the team agreed on some easily digestible values to communicate the new way of doing things:

- Know your stuff (emphasis on product knowledge and personal development).
- Don't wait to be asked (encourages initiative and problem solving).
- Make it feel special (customer focus and team leadership).
- Treat people like family (supportive, helpful, friendly).

These values are very employee-specific and describe the practical ways that LV= will achieve the vision of becoming a top five national insurance organization.

The point about the diversity of these examples is to emphasize that your vision should be unique to your organization and that it can probably only work for you. In these days of internet-based information it would be easy to wordsearch the values of the leading global organizations and simply choose those that seem to go together and sound elegant and inspiring. But it would not work. Only you know what your employees, customers and distributors will perceive as being both doable and authentic. There is no 'one-size-fits-all' when it comes to vision and values. It is interesting to note that most organizations that have any stated values at all tend to have three or four core values and certainly no more than five.

'Envisioned future'

Some consultants who regularly assist large organizations in articulating a new vision and set of values add another element, sometimes known as the 'envisioned future'. In other words there should be an expression of a major goal that reaches into the next 30 years or so and there may be a bold statement attached to it. So, rather than keeping your feet on the ground, why not go for a big challenge and see what happens? Some examples are:

Nike.   To be the number one athletic company in the world.

Pfizer.   We will become the world's most valued company to patients, customers, colleagues, investors, business partners, and the communities where we work and live.

Volkswagen.   By 2018 the Volkswagen Group is to be the world's most successful and fascinating automobile manufacturer – and the leading light when it comes to sustainability.

Agreeing the vision and values

Changing the way any organization goes about its daily processes is not easy, so it would be remarkable if thinking up a new vision and corresponding values would be achieved in a few days or even a few months. It should also be borne in mind that organizational politics plays its part. The role of the CEO, or whoever is leading your organization, is crucial in setting the tone of the debate as is being able, as a senior group, to reach a considered conclusion that is not just agreeing to adopt whatever the leader says. We will look at the importance of leadership in the next chapter, but for now this is how you might successfully conduct a revision of current values and the timescales involved:

1 Gather the market and employee information about perceptions as described above and ensure that it is easily digestible by senior executives from different disciplines.

2 Choose a suitable change management consultant or team, preferably external to avoid bias, and give them full sight of all the research.

3 Hold an initial scoping session to agree the range of issues to be discussed with your consultant and set some objectives.

4 Convene the team (it may be that this team is not necessarily the existing senior team, you may add operations people or long-serving employees) and take them through the problem (we need to change) and how we are going to do it (through a new vision and set of values).

5 Set aside plenty of time to discuss the vision. This could be a few hours but more likely an away day or two depending on the complexity of your organization. For an international business it may be a series of senior meetings to get buy-in to the process and articulation of the vision.

6 Allow breathing space for various departments and divisions to think through what the vision means to them from an operational viewpoint. This could be a few weeks or even months.

7 Publish a set of values and engage lower levels of operational employees to discuss how these values might work and whether they truly reflect or could reflect a revitalized organization.

8 Revise the values and begin the process of planning how to communicate them to all employees, distributors and consumers.

You will find this process both rewarding and frustrating. Depending on how traditional the existing organization is, you may find it hard to get employees to tell you what they really think, as hierarchy and deference play a big part in organizational life. Use the consultant to filter out feedback that is self-serving or too respectful. Equally, some senior colleagues may feel they cannot be 'honest' about some change issues if it means they have to change. Getting people to be part of the solution rather than the problem is a skill in itself, and the natural order of things may need to be suspended for the purposes of getting the vision and values right.

CASE STUDY   Barclays Bank values

The banking sector has had a difficult time in recent years regarding consumer trust. The original financial crisis that started in the sub-prime housing sector in the United States helped to trigger the Euro crisis and was not helped by local crises in the UK, such as the scandal over the fixing of the LIBOR inter-bank lending rate and a major mis-selling of personal insurance. Consequently UK consumer trust in financial services was at an all-time low in the early part of 2013. Following various changes of senior management at Barclays Bank the incoming Group Chief Executive, Anthony Jenkins, announced that there would be a new set of values for the organization. He announced a new vision, called 'purpose':

Purpose: *Helping people achieve their ambitions – in the right way.*

To support this new vision or purpose he then announced five new 'values and behaviours' which were intended to guide employees in their dealings with each other, with customers and with the various channels they sold through. The five values were:

1 Respect.

2 Integrity.

3 Service.

4 Excellence.

5 Stewardship.

Each of these values had a sub-set of explanatory phrases designed to help employees apply the rather abstract values being promoted. For example 'respect' was followed by:

We respect and value those we work with, and the contribution that they make.

- Build trust with the colleagues and partners we work with.

- Seek out alternative perspectives and put our shared interests ahead of any individual or team.

- Collaborate proactively with colleagues across all of Barclays to get the best results.

- Embrace, and seek to increase, the diversity of our organization.

You can see how the main vision has been broken down into no more than five key values and each of those values has been further broken down into more detailed guidance on how this applies in the workplace. You can imagine in the employee briefings how much further these phrases would be broken down to make them relevant to whichever team was being briefed.

In terms of keeping the communication consistent, on the day that the new values were announced the Chief Executive made himself available to the national media for interviews. The television coverage revealed a simple backdrop behind the speaker which displayed just the five values in big letters, no other words or graphics. These values were clearly visible on all the news bulletins broadcast on that launch day. In this way the consumer, the channel partners and the employees all saw the same message at the same time, adding to the authenticity and credibility of the announcement. If you add to this the fact that Andrew Jenkins gave up his substantial annual banker's bonus as a gesture of apology, it all begins to come together as an organization that understands strategic brand engagement and how the vision and values need to be crafted as one piece with as little jargon as possible.

HR and marketing working together

It may seem an obvious point, but not so obvious when you look at some of the convoluted and wordy 'values' that are often promoted on websites, that HR and marketing need to work together. This is particularly true in the crafting of the words. Too often the writing of such an important statement of new intent is handed down from a small core of senior managers without recourse to communications specialists. Most heads of business tend to have a financial or technical background, which makes them ill-suited to creating acceptable word patterns that everyone can understand, so it makes sense to ask marketing to come up with acceptable terminology and for HR to moderate any possible whiff of marketing-speak when it comes to crafting the new message for employees.

The vision may be short or long but it has to work across employees, distributors and consumers so some thought needs to be given to its transparency when used in different communication situations. A message to employees to be 'cost-effective' may not go down well with the channel that is looking for service from its business partners. In the same way consumers may perceive your brand to be of high quality for all kinds of historic reasons but that image would be inconsistent with employees whose main mantra is cost-consciousness. It is likely that you will be communicating in open media online so you can never assume that what you say to employees will not be seen by the channel or the general media. The chances are it will, so all variations of the core message need to be consistent and 'authentic'.

Avoid marketing-speak

For large organizations it is all too easy to slip into 'consultant-speak' and start to use phrases that have little or no meaning for those who are not privy to the discussions of the inner sanctum. It is perfectly acceptable to write out the vision and values using technical jargon initially. But you need to be inclusive enough to let marketing people and professional communicators be sceptical about the words being used and for you to be challenged by 'outsiders' as to what they actually mean. To some extent this is where strategic brand engagement starts. Whatever you come up with it needs to speak to employees, the channel and consumers. If it needs to be 'translated' once published, then the job has not been done properly. The chairman's wife test is still a valid, if slightly sexist, one. If she does not understand what it means, the chances are that no one else will either and unless you are the chairman's wife, few people lower down the hierarchy will have the courage to challenge the senior team as to what it really means. Nobody wants to be made to look a fool in front of their colleagues so their silence could well be taken as comprehension... which is usually not the case.

In the same way that the master brand has sub-brands, so the values may well have sub-expressions of those values depending on the type of employee or distributor being asked to engage with your brand. Without wishing to make too many assumptions it may be that divisional managers have a different set of explanatory notes to retail part-timers. For example, if one of the values is 'our customers deserve to receive top quality service' this needs to be communicated to divisional managers to cover the need for relevant skills training to deliver this, and for how it applies to internal colleagues. For retail part-timers this value would emphasize what 'top quality service' means in terms of behaviour and response attitudes when face-to-face with a consumer.

Nothing is forever

It may seem odd to say that just because you have set a big, bold vision for the next 30 years (envisioning the future), that does not mean you cannot change it again in five or 10 years' time. The market, technology and social trends change all the time so organizational vision and values will also need to change. Sony in the 1950s published a vision that stated it wanted to become 'the company most known for changing the worldwide poor-quality image of Japanese products'. Now, 60 years later, its stated vision is: 'To create exciting new digital entertainment experiences for consumers by bringing together cutting-edge products with latest generation content and services.'

You could well find yourself doing the same thing several times for the same organization as the world changes around it. Some might say the key to organizational longevity is its ability to reinvent itself as and when the need arises. There are very few long-lasting, iconic organizations that always get it right all of the time; they number in the hundreds globally rather than in the thousands.

The engagement brand book

The practical output from all these deliberations is a vision and values 'brand book'. This is a detailed, step-by-step guide that breaks down all the promises and claims into practical steps for each audience and by definition for every employee. This may seem unnecessarily fussy, but it will be needed because managers have to know what the new messages are and how they should be interpreted. Rather than be overly prescriptive about what the interpretations should be, part of the new ethos of 'trust' involves asking managers to meet together to agree what it means for them. This is normally achieved through a series of guided workshops, resulting in an agreed approach, with variations for certain types of employee group.

DHL, the global logistics organization now owned by Deutschepost, undertook a thorough overhaul of its employer brand in 2009, resulting in a restatement of its core employer brand values, which were:

- personal commitment;
- proactive solutions;
- local strength worldwide.

These key values were then broken down into dozens of everyday behaviours that demonstrate the key values, as applied to specific employee groups and published in the DHL Brand Book. In the same way that the consumer brand has guidelines that marketing people can consult, so do managers and employees. Taking this concept further it is simple to see how compliance with the new engagement 'brand book guidelines' could then become the basis for appraisals, recognition and reward to complete the virtuous circle of vision, values and changed behaviour.

Questioning values is an ongoing process

Whether the vision and values remain for five years or five decades, the process of questioning whether people are engaging with the brand is what will enable you to continue to be successful. To assume that you will always be successful, without questioning current engagement levels is a guaranteed way to go out of business fast.

How organizations behave is often based on what comes from the top. Even global enterprises are managed by a few key individuals who imbue the rest of the organization with their way of working, for good or bad. For that reason the importance of sound leadership cannot be underestimated. In the next chapter we explore what good leadership looks like and why it can have such a crucial effect on the way an organization engages with its various audiences.

Leading brand engagement

05

Employee engagement means opening up decision making and change to those who will add value, not faster more persuasive propaganda. (SMYTHE, 2007)

It would be a mistake to think that once the vision and values have been agreed, all you need to do as a senior manager or leader is to promote the agenda aggressively, adding a few incentives along the way to reward higher compliance and recognize the top performers. Then you can get on with business as usual, which is, of course, all about higher revenues and lower costs – or so it would appear in many organizations. But brand engagement only works if there is employee trust. Trust cannot be won through good internal marketing alone, although it undoubtedly helps. Leaders need to be seen to be involved, to be actually leading the programme and, above all, to be trusted. Trust is the most important issue when values and behaviours are analysed, so being able to buy into what the leaders in the business say and do is the lead indicator when it comes to measuring strategic brand engagement.

What is leadership?

Let's deal first with what leadership actually is. In the view of Charles Handy (1999) leaders are born not made (trait theory); this has largely been discredited or not yet proven. That leaves style and contingency theories. By contingency he suggests that situations throw up leaders for certain situations and then they fade into the background when they are no longer needed. There seems to be a lot of sense in this idea. But it is of little use to organizational planners who want to be able to choose good leaders before the situation arises. For that reason the most useful predictor of effective leadership is style – in other words, a person's way of handling people when specific leadership situations arise.

There are dozens of styles of leadership, depending on how far you want to drill down into the differences. The ability to lead is a continuum with very poor at one end and very good at the other. It also seems that styles vary from highly autocratic to highly democratic. But contingency theory tells us that often leadership skills vary with the situation. Financial leadership is a very different skill to emotional leadership. Unless the organization is in some kind of resources crisis financial leadership is the least likely style to win the hearts and minds of the workforce when markets are stable. People buy into visions not volumes. Lewin, in the 1940s, first promoted the idea that there were three basic styles of leadership: authoritarian, democratic (participative) or delegative (*laissez-faire*). Researchers found that children in classrooms, for example, under delegative leadership, were the least productive of all three groups; they also made more demands on the leader, showed little co-operation and were unable to work independently. This does not suggest you should never delegate. But you should not always delegate in every organizational situation – it's a judgment call. Sometimes you just have to step up to the plate and take a decision if a deadline is approaching.

Gayle Lantz, president of Workplace Inc, a human resources consulting firm in Birmingham, AL, uses the popular DISC assessment tool as part of her practice to identify four main leadership styles; they are the conductor, the influencer, the supporter and the analyser. It could be said that 'the analyser' has simply been added to Lewin's original leadership types. Analysers tend to do nothing until all the available research has been conducted and the consequences of making changes have been tested. This works well in multinational, long-term businesses where consensus is the order of the day, but it is less effective in a fast-moving, smaller type of business where the market changes faster than the process of getting internal agreement.

The Hay Group suggests there may be six distinct leadership styles:

1 coercive;

2 authoritative;

3 affiliative;

4 democratic;

5 pacesetting; and

6 coaching.

Famous historical names are often cited to support the various styles as being either a good thing or a bad thing. In the context of a business 'affiliative' means promoting harmony and friendship – a leader who does not like to rock the boat and likes to keep everyone happy, as far as possible. But everyday organizational life rarely provides the opportunity to be Churchill, Mao Tse-tung or JFK. Complications begin when some consultants suggest that you can adapt your style to different audiences. When all the styles of leadership have been analysed, across all given situations, they broadly fall into dictatorial at one end of the spectrum and collaborative at the other. You could say that in times of stress, such as war, a dictatorial style is the most effective. In times of peace, collaboration is the key. It is also true that styles change depending on the gravity of the situation or the need to act quickly. But in the context of employee brand engagement we need a style that suits agreement, inclusion, affiliation and delegation. This is not a moral issue: it just happens to be more effective working this way in the post-internet world where information is freely shared and joint enterprise works better than single, authoritarian endeavour.

Because effective leadership is a key component of employee engagement it is worth spending some time thinking about what effective leadership is and how different leadership styles impact on engagement. It is unrealistic to expect all leaders to behave the same way at all times. But all leaders need to realize that their style can seriously undermine attempts to improve enterprise engagement. So perhaps leadership 'style' within the closed doors of the top floor suite may need to be modified so as not to undo all the good work on the admin floor that a transition towards proper employee engagement requires.

Theory X leadership

Thanks to Douglas McGregor back in the 1960s most people in organizations now see the folly of being a Theory X leader. Theory X leaders are target-driven, prefer coercion to collaboration and sincerely believe employees are motivated by money alone, would rather shirk than work and need to be pushed and coerced into higher performance. This technique can work, over the short term, in a crisis, when perhaps a deadline needs to be hit or a process problem resolved. But it becomes increasingly difficult to achieve higher performance or retain good employees using the stick approach all the time. It is also inefficient. The costs of losing good people and having to recruit a new team are substantial, and there may be issues of employment and contract rights.

In Theory X organizations new ideas and changes in process are expected to come from 'the top', which results in employees not being innovative and 'waiting' for the management hierarchy to solve all their problems; it therefore becomes expensive (time is money) to change things. The Theory X strategy for engagement would be to delegate the implementation of the new values through the hierarchical chain of management and move on to, in their view, more pressing organizational tasks, such as saving costs and making more money.

Unfortunately this is the authoritarian model that probably still describes the vast majority of organizations in the developed world and has been in use for a long time. More recently employees have questioned its assumptions, as have more enlightened employers. The idea that power is based on information held by a select few is outdated, when most information is now in the public domain, thanks to the internet. Real power lies in the effective communication of such information, not simply being the gatekeeper of it.

Theory Y leaders trust employees

Theory Y leaders value involvement from employees, perceive that they need to participate rather than be merely 'victims' of change and appreciate that employees want to be involved and to do a good job. In McGregor's world Theory Y leaders allow team members to be confident in their own ability to solve the day-to-day problems of organizational life. They understand that employees often have useful things to say about the bigger, more strategic issues as well. He mentions Theory Y leaders being perceived as 'being fair' to employees and having 'upwards influence'. All this adds up to building a bond of trust between employee and leader. This in turn leads to higher levels of active engagement by employees in terms of being told the 'truth' about any changes and their leader having enough clout to be able to manage problems up the line rather than just accepting the way things are.

There is no simple list of dos and don'ts to gaining trust, as every organizational situation is unique. But most academic studies and consultancies would probably agree on the following criteria for a leader to be trusted:

- Involve employees in the creation and development of any new strategies/processes.
- Communicate the overall objectives in a succinct and simple manner.
- Show behaviours that are consistent with the new plan/vision.
- Have values that are consistent with the overall vision of the organization.
- Behave in a positive and enthusiastic manner.

Charles Green wrote in *Forbes* magazine in March 2012:

> Sending a leader into today's world armed with only the vertical, power-based skills of the past is like sending a Civil War soldier into modern battle. The leadership weapon of the future is trust – a change so profound that it invalidates the 'weapon' metaphor itself. Winning with trust is different; it's not a zero-sum game. We all benefit from it.

But it is almost impossible to be consistent at all times in every situation. There may be a higher outcome at stake that is beyond the control of junior employees. It may be that the key discussion has already taken place and a decision to change things has already gone beyond the consultative phase. There may be times when implementing new procedures has to be carried out without discussion, although explaining why this has to be so in any particular case would go a long way to retaining employee trust. But in general, on most occasions a good leader would have the behavioural traits described above and have earned enough trust to be able to push through a dramatic change if the need arose, with the minimum of consultation.

True engagement needs an engaged leadership

In 2004 Towers Perrin, the consultancy firm, analysed the main drivers of engagement and underlined the informal perception that to be engaged senior managers need to have a sincere and authentic interest in employee wellbeing. In other words, they instinctively see the value in reducing the fear that inhibits traditional organizations and look to provide an atmosphere of collaboration and respect. The second driver of an engaged workforce is that senior managers lead by example in demonstrating organizational values. A further study in 2005 conducted by Melcrum Publishing put 'leadership' as one of the top three drivers of engagement, with 20 per cent stating that they had difficulty in getting senior managers to take owner-ship of engagement initiatives, once they had been agreed.

If you need a checklist of what leaders need to do to improve engagement within their organizations and direct teams effectively it would probably include the following:

- Trust and be trusted by your own team... and other teams.
- Communicate a clear vision, when the need arises.
- Involve team members in decisions that will affect them directly.
- Take opportunities to build self-respect and esteem amongst team members.
- Show you support organizational values.
- Monitor engagement and discuss the findings with employees.
- Respond to feedback and do not ignore negative comments.
- Build a work ethic that is enjoyable and fulfilling for team members.

To do this successfully at all times with all the upwards and downwards pressures that crowd in on most managers is a tough call. But as an engaged leader at least you know what people want to see, even if it is not possible to deliver it on every occasion. Nigel Nicholson (2013) in his book *The 'I' of Leadership* ('I' = eye) stresses the point that the best perceived leaders are those who exhibit 'seeing' skills:

> Seeing is the key. Reframe safety as threat, danger as opportunity, desire as dependence and people can switch their goals and actions in a flash... People need to see the logic of the journey and be reassured that if the future is not going to be like the past it is connected in ways that are part of the story.

Smythe's power-sharing model

So, assuming you agree that being a Theory Y leader/manager is more effective than simply bossing people about, how would a Theory Y leader normally go about getting cooperation from the team, whether that is a decision-making board or a group of telesales people? Traditionally leaders have followed a recognizable way of working to decide how much (or how little) to involve employees in decision making, knowingly or not. John Smythe and colleagues (see Smythe, 2007) developed one of the first published models as part of an employee research project; see Figure 5.1.

FIGURE 5.1 Engaging with employees

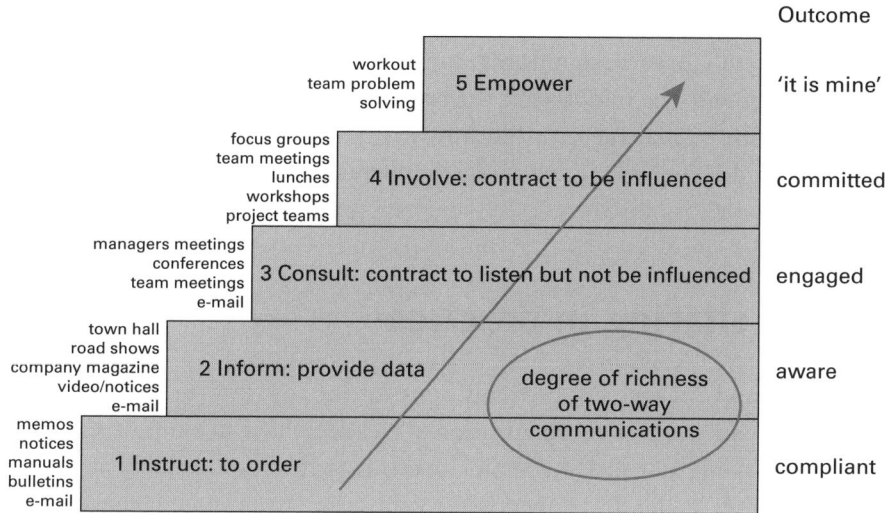

SOURCE: Smythe, 2007

At the lowest level you can disseminate information via e-mail and put a poster on an employee notice board. This assumes that employees will simply comply with what is being proposed. This is ideal for non-controversial instructions and procedures where no agreement is necessary and may just be an activity that everyone agrees with because it is the obvious thing to do. The second level is making people aware of a new situation or fact and this could be done through a video briefing or official publication... again no interaction or feedback is sought directly. The third level is to hold a team briefing or a conference where delegates listen rather than actively feed back suggestions or improvements. The fourth level is to set up a focus group or meeting where the sponsors are deliberately asking for input. The top level is presenting all the facts and asking those who will be affected to participate in the implications or the problems the new scenario may create in the future.

As you can see down the right-hand side, each of the techniques has a direct outcome in the eyes of the participant. Engagement, albeit passive, occurs only at level three and absolute ownership of the issue by employees only happens at level five. The strategic brand engagement suggestion is to start the engagement process much earlier on, working from level three upwards rather than relying on offering the information in a fairly anonymous manner.

That means even straightforward decisions about processes should be discussed by the team and implemented by them with little or no interference from management. It means managers can concentrate on the bigger issues that will have a significant impact on successful outcomes rather than dealing with the minutiae of the organization. We can all recognize the dangers of micro-management but how many of us make a conscious decision not to do it when we see things happening to a process that we may not agree with?

Power sharing in practice

Leading brand engagement certainly starts at the top. But for such a policy to be successful across the organization all 'leaders' have to embrace the new way of working, not just the senior team. It is the responsibility of every manager, team leader and supervisor to subscribe to brand engagement or the good work of the few may well be negated by the indifferent work of many.

It has to be recognized that some leaders may still see 'engagement' as a technical way to align employees with the organization's goals. If so, it does nothing more than support hierarchy models of 'command and control' – it's just another way to coerce employees into complying with what the senior team have already decided they want to get done. Engagement needs to be a way to open up decision-making to the widest possible group of employees.

But decisions do not happen in isolation. The original and unique values of the organization need to be well-learnt by team leaders so that when it comes to choosing A or B as a way of solving a problem they have some agreed foundations on which to base a decision. For example, if one of your values is 'challenging the status quo' then a team leader who does not look at alternative processes to delivering quality is not engaging with the brand in an authentic way and employees will be the first to spot this.

Personal challenges

Making values personal to every organizational situation means that individual team leaders will begin to apply the new model in both big and small situations to the extent that being aware of the brand then becomes highly personal. No longer do they see 'policy' as something that is delivered from the top of the organization: it is a shared way of doing things that they can introduce at lower and middle levels and follow through with. If a change in process needs to be made, team leaders are then empowered to decide what change would fit best with the new values and be free to discuss such changes with team members before implementing them. Naturally, from time to time, they may get it wrong technically or may not have thought through the cost implications of a change in process. But mistakes are okay within the strategic brand engagement paradigm: you can always go back and fix it later. That is better than not fixing it at all because you are waiting on instructions from above – which may never happen because the top is not aware there is a problem.

Transformational leadership

Challenging the process, inspiring a shared vision, enabling others to act, modelling the way, encouraging the heart. These are the components of the Kouzes and Posner (2009) model of transformational leadership which, they argued, is compatible with the new workforce that is now largely Generation Y or the Millennials – those born from about 1980 onwards (see Figure 10.1 on page 148). When Douglas Coupland used the phrase 'Generation X' in his seminal novel in 1991 he wrote about the generation who came after the post-war Baby Boomers who were no longer satisfied to simply toe the establishment line and accept the way things were. They grew up in a time of turmoil and protest and witnessed the invention of the personal computer, the internet and mobile telephony. Their future was to be more collaborative and individualistic. Their legacy, Generation Y, was that their own children were encouraged not to conform, to communicate with their peers on what seems like a minute-by-minute basis and to find it normal that information and data are instant and not something you wait for to be provided by someone else, or behave deferentially to acquire. Today's workforce is unlikely to simply take instructions and carry them out without questioning their validity.

For leaders in today's organizations it's not enough to give orders anymore. Employees expect to be consulted about changes before they are made (information is instant so why not just let us see it?) and to be able to discuss the implications. Engagement is all about inviting collaboration rather than dictating policies. It could be described as a new, power-sharing approach which is more bottom-up than top-down. People still need leadership in this context but it is a listening and enabling style of leadership rather than a controlling one.

Transformation in this sense does not imply some kind of superhero leader who dispenses values and direction at random following a flash of inspiration. It is a description of a group of agreed actions that lead to dramatic business change. It is argued that implementing such change can be learnt and then applied to any organization, so you do not need to be a natural transformational leader to apply it.

The case of Jordanian Schools

One of the best explanations of transformational leadership in practice is outlined by Kouzes and Posner (2009). Using over 20 years' research into leadership styles, Kouzes and Posner put forward the idea that leaders above all should be disruptive in the sense of not accepting the situation as it is and be courageous enough to introduce new ideas and paradigms. But simply being 'unpredictable' and wanting to change everything does not do the job. There has to be a method in it for it to work as a business or organizational tool.

The idea behind their Jordanian Schools case study was to determine to what degree schoolteachers thought their principals and government administrators exhibited the five principles outlined below, with a view to identifying improvements in certain areas through coaching. It just so happens that in this study their supervisors scored highest on 'enabling others to act' but lowest on 'inspiring a shared vision'. In other words there is a suggestion here that teachers get no steer from their education department about the higher values of education in Jordan and are largely taking local decisions in the absence of any higher mission or set of values. The important point is that this type of organization has set a benchmark that shows where the gaps in leadership skills exist and is now able to work on those gaps to improve them. A crucial takeaway is that, regardless of the facts, this is how the school teachers perceived their leaders to be, rather than possibly how they really behaved. Leadership is all about the perceptions of them by those who are being led. Just like the brand, leaders are largely effective as a result of the level of trust employees place in them. Ordering people about just does not cut it anymore.

First principle

The first principle for a leader is to challenge all organizational processes. Look for ways to support innovation, change the accepted way of doing things, take risks, try new markets, try new methods and make mistakes if necessary. An absence of a blame culture will free up executives to learn from errors rather than play it safe. It goes without saying that those who do make mistakes should be protected from dismissal and not redeployed into less important parts of the organization, as this would send completely the wrong signals to upcoming Generation Y employees who are themselves progressing through the business. Mistakes should be seen as opportunities to learn rather than situations to be avoided the next time something needs to be challenged.

Second principle

The second principle is to create and inspire a 'shared vision'. This emphasis takes us back to 'envisioning the future' and outlining where the organization is heading. The general mood is positive and hopeful, rather than conservative and defensive. Using good communication techniques and being upbeat supports the shared vision approach.

Third principle

From these two principles collaboration and empowerment follow. The atmosphere of trust in employees to do the right thing means that much of the detailed planning of the organization can be carried out by them, not the senior team. This leads to a general feeling that employees 'own' the organization and have the power to correct anomalies and change things if the current policy is not working. In one sense the senior team are there to provide the resources for success rather than make all the key decisions – collaborative rather than coercive.

Fourth principle

The fourth principle is 'modelling the way'. Employees need to know that there is a path and that it leads somewhere better, different, more enjoyable. Any set of standards or values is measured and everyone knows if they fall short. But there is a discernible emphasis away from financial targets towards behavioural targets. These values should be seen to be upheld by the senior team and not just used as some kind of magic formula that only applies to lower level employees. Authenticity is the key: there is no point in espousing the new values in public if in private with your colleagues you are bemoaning the fact that revenue is down and someone needs to be let go.

You have to trust the brand engagement process. There should be clear consistency between what leaders preach as the desired way of working and how they work themselves. Mutual respect and being authentic would sum it up, regardless of perceived hierarchy.

Fifth principle

The last principle is described in the report as 'encouraging the heart'. For some people this may sound a little soft and 'new age', but it does recognize that employees are people too and that they need to be recognized and rewarded as human beings for doing a good job. Leaders should be seen to be involved in this process by hosting lunches, allowing themselves to be promoted throughout the organization as good role models, encouraging a sense of belonging and teamwork.

The Chief Engagement Officer

Smythe coined the term 'The Chief Engagement Officer' in 2007 to make the point that all leaders, managers and supervisors should now have an additional task: 'The job description involves being responsible for ensuring the planning and execution of the engagement of their people in day-to-day performance and change.'

In essence this means considering how to engage colleagues in decision-making, not just at the end when the decision has been taken but from the very beginning. Leaders should consider who could add value to the discussion of the options, how to explore a shared story of possible outcomes, who might be useful in communicating it, how it is to be communicated and reviewing what happened as a result of the decision. It's a team approach. For traditionalists this sounds as if it could take much longer than just telling people what to do. But the world has moved on and in the long run engagement as a technique to get things done through others is more efficient than doing it yourself. Information is no longer exclusively held in the hands of senior managers and when everyone has the knowledge then knowledge is no longer power, organizationally speaking.

Brand engagement leadership

If we agree that engagement-style leadership requires a different view of the world to old-style, dictatorial, command and control, what are the implications for leading brand engagement?

Brand engagement includes taking into account the customers' experience when they engage with the organization. This suggests that there is a leadership role for customer champions or internal 'ambassadors' to lead the organization on specific processes, however small. For example, someone who is known for turning irate customers who want to complain into firm advocates could be used to train teams in other parts of the process, such as the legal department, finance or procurement.

There may be distributors who are so good at selling your products independently (you know who they are from your data records) that they could lead the development of internal sales skills, and help them become even more aligned to your brand by helping to shape how the brand is delivered internally. Conversely, it would be in the organization's interest to coach promising distributor staff in team working and leadership skills, even though they are not on your payroll. This is common practice in formal, technical product sessions but few offer to 'develop' distributors' managerial skills so that in partnership with your organization they become a better, more effective business partner for your organization. With distributors and the organization 'singing off the same hymn-sheet' brand values would be easier to assimilate so customers get the same brand message, rather than a watered-down version of the original concept they have seen on the internet or on TV.

How to lead... the future

There has been some dissatisfaction in recent years with the individual-centric coaching of leaders. With flatter and flatter structures, remote working and collaborative networking with other independent organizations and partners it is clear that the better-performing leaders are those who favour 'collective' leadership. That means leading through collaboration, moving from one good idea to another without long gaps for internal evaluation, forming and reforming action teams on a regular basis, and creating new ways of achieving tasks that do not depend on a fixed group of employees or a fixed cadre of 'leaders'.

Another important and effective element of good practice leadership is nurturing and encouraging the emergence of project leaders for specific tasks and allowing them to fade into the background when the task is over. Good leaders could be anywhere in the organization and they do not necessarily need to be on a 'fast-track' programme or destined for a senior career. In some instances they could be from outside your organization and because of their objectivity they may well be just right for the task you want completed.

Finally, removing fear to create 'freedom-centred' leadership should be the goal of all successful organizations of the future. It should be okay to make a mistake, to take a few wrong turns, to try a new idea... even if you have done something similar before and it did not work. All these ideas live happily together within a well-engaged organization that is comfortable with its brand and whose employees trust both each other and their leaders.

It is obvious from this that, on the macro level, leadership of the change towards an engaged culture requires knowledge of people issues and sufficient skill in handling them as well as a professional acquaintance with marketing communications. The 'Chief Engagement Officer' does not necessarily need to be the top leader in the business. But he or she does need to be respected at the highest level for a thorough understanding of the people and comms issues that flow from going down the brand engagement road.

Good leadership is the most important driver

Much has been written about identifying the particular drivers of effective employee engagement. These drivers are often not universal and range from the general to the specific, depending on the organization: people working well in teams, input into decisions, clear vision from above, having career progression, being trusted, sector-standard benefits, etc. But of all these, the most important and most commonly cited wish from employees in many benchmark studies over the years is for quality leadership. By 'quality' we do not just mean leaders who know the theory and are seen to be effective in a crisis. Leaders who engage have a personal style which is employee-centric and is consistent throughout their dealings with employees and the wider world. When they talk to the media they often say 'we' rather than 'I' and are seen to show confidence in their workforce rather than simply satisfaction in the numbers that the C-suite team has produced.

If a VP talks about the need to engage and involve but takes his lunch in the Executive Suite and insists on being known by his surname or even worse, by some title ('Sir John'), it breaks the rule of authenticity for most Generation Y employees. We cannot 'all be in this together' if the senior team lead separate lives and rarely, if ever, walk the floors and talk to employees about doing the basic tasks on which the organization's success depends.

Nearly ready to implement? Not quite. Before we embark on any change programme we need to make sure that we have set a benchmark for success. There will be plenty of naysayers out there who will be looking for reasons not to 'get with the programme' because they feel comfortable with the way things are. So the next chapter deals with how to measure engagement and, more importantly, how to interpret the results.

Measuring strategic brand engagement

06

> *Surveying helps you establish where you are now versus where you want to be.* (SARAH COOK, 2008)

With the importance of leadership behaviour understood and brand values to some extent sorted or rather re-sorted for now, the next step is to move forward and implement an engagement plan. But nothing should happen without putting a stake in the ground about where the organization stands right now in terms of its levels of engagement with employees, customers and the channel.

In the performance improvement industry the beneficial connection between goal-setting, performance measurement and feedback is known as 'measure-monitor-mirror'. In short this means setting a performance benchmark, measuring any change going forward and ensuring that performance is fed back to participants in a way they can relate to. The idea is that people perform better if you give them personal feedback about how they are doing, even if they are not doing that well. The first element of measurement therefore is establishing a starting point for performance from which everything else flows.

First, you need to establish an initial performance benchmark so that at the very least you can measure any improvement going forward. There's no point in spending lots of time and executive effort to construct a huge engagement roll-out exercise if you do not know where you are starting from. It would be too easy for naysayers to claim, after the fact, that things were ok anyway and all we needed was a better economy with rising employment. In classic marketing terms what you need is some top-line research on which to base your communication plans and set a benchmark for future success and improvements. In addition, as we intend to build a strategic brand engagement programme we need to factor in consumer perceptions of the brand as well as what the channel thinks about your brand. But most engagement initiatives start with the employees. So, let's survey them first.

Master of all you survey

We have already established in an earlier chapter that levels of engagement vary across economies, organizations and even within organizations themselves. Although in theory the drivers of engagement would seem to be constant, in practice it depends on what job is being done by employees and what relationship those in the survey have with the overall organization. It is easy to see that the mature management cadre of a long-established multinational who are 'on the inside track' of corporate information are more likely to be highly engaged than junior clerical staff who may have only been employed for a few years. In terms of expectations, various surveys show that employee groups are generally engaged anywhere between 40 and 80 per cent, with the 'highly engaged' numbering only about 15 per cent of the total. This means that in most organizations there is still plenty of room for improvement. The important thing is to *improve* your engagement level rather than just congratulate yourself on any absolute figure.

In our earlier example, the UK general insurance organization LV= went from a benchmark figure of 64 per cent engagement prior to any sustained effort in 2007 to an overall score of 83 per cent in 2011, following organization-wide initiatives. That is an increase of 19 percentage points. It demonstrates that although 64 per cent engagement is not bad, there was considerable scope for improvement with all the financial benefits that such improvements could bring to the organization.

LV= was particularly concerned to be scoring higher than the sector average as the employee market for good administrative employees is highly competitive and employees often ask how employers rate on scores of employee satisfaction and overall engagement. In LV='s case the average for the sector was 70 per cent so it now operates in the top quartile for engagement for the kind of employees it wants to attract.

Proprietary surveys

In Chapter 2 we briefly discussed general survey findings about engagement from employee support and research organizations such as Gallup, The Hay Group and Towers Perrin. There are, of course, many others and some specialize in certain market sectors, such as the Institute of Employment Services, which surveys the UK National Health Service. The value of such surveys is that they are relatively inexpensive for large organizations to take part in and provide a statistically valid measure of comparative engagement because they survey many thousands of employees who are similar to the profile of their employees. But a single headline figure rarely takes into account the whole story.

As with all outsourced services you need to make sure that the findings are used as a guideline for your own bespoke activity and not as prescriptive. All organizations are unique, so a general survey will only give you a general indication of what is happening in your own organization during a particular period in comparison with other organizations. A recent merger or change in the profile of your employees could explain any sudden deviations from past performance scores, so any dramatic changes should be viewed sceptically, until you can uncover the underlying reasons for the change.

One example is the general trend towards disengagement of the under-35s within the Western world, as evidenced in a number of country surveys. This is an important generic finding as it impacts on local engagement programmes where the assumption that all are engaged to an equal degree is false. If you have a large, youngish group of employees, often known as Generation Y, (born between 1981 and 2000) they will have a different view of their employer than older, more established employees. Vineet Nayar, author of *Employees First, Customers Second* (2010) puts it succinctly:

> Unlike the longer-serving employees... these younger people weren't impressed that I was president. They didn't care so much about titles and positions, they didn't look for upward direction. They believed in collaboration, they loved to learn. They shared everything... music, information, ideas, feelings.

So demographics can play an important part in how employees report about themselves. For instance, 40 per cent engagement from an employee group of part-time students working in the distribution warehouse for the summer may be as good as it gets, no matter what intervention you may decide to implement. Forty per cent engagement from long-term managers who often get involved in corporate planning and management change programmes should be deeply worrying.

If you are buying into generic surveys, you may need to factor in 'country differences' for engagement measures. The Global Employee Engagement Index is an international benchmark tool from the research organization Effectory that provides insights into work perception, worldwide. The index shows how different countries score on the 17 most important HR topics, and enables global HR-professionals (of complex organizational structures) to perform more efficiently and effectively. Broadly speaking the United States is pretty near the top globally, while South Africa scores very poorly when measuring engagement issues. Of course there may be valid reasons for these overall scores; possibly the maturity of the workforce, and their familiarity with the engagement concept within an organizational context, will contribute to a higher score than those who have never been involved in such a programme before.

Another factor is what industry sector the organization belongs to. In recent years engagement scores in the telecommunications sector have been one of the lowest overall, but professional services and education are always one of the highest. Government legislation and other political factors can also play a major part in raising average business sector engagement scores: generally speaking the more professional and technical the organization, the more likely that engagement will be high. When barriers to entry are low, with many part-timers and possibly commission-only remuneration, engagement tends to be low, so it would be unrealistic to expect energy sector salespeople on commission to be as well engaged as, say, surgeons. All survey results need to be seen in their appropriate market context.

New recruits

Many organizations use three years' service as a useful cut-off point for data so that you can compare 'new joiners' versus 'established employees' across all the findings. Over time this can provide a useful measure of attitude change as new recruits become established contributors to the organizational good. But beware of having relatively unimportant issues being flagged up as requiring 'urgent attention'. As all senior managers know it is too easy to be buttonholed by an employee at an internal event about a specific issue and be fooled into thinking it needs immediate, strategic attention. Clearly if any employees have an axe to grind they should be taken seriously, but their comments should always be seen in the context of what most people in their demographic actually think is a serious, organization-wide issue.

Survey your own values

It would be a mistake to think that all you need to do is subscribe to a generic engagement survey from one of the big survey organizations and consider the job done. Some argue that generic benchmarking is only there for senior teams to pat themselves on the back. John Smythe, author of *The Chief Engagement Officer* (2007), is less than complimentary:

> Benchmarking seems to appeal most to competitive leaders who are more concerned with their own vanity than the needs and drivers of their people... most employee research benchmarking sheds little light on solutions and practices... but I agree that comparisons may act as a spur to leaders to do things better and that is useful.

Although many generic benchmarking surveys have been tried and tested over the years and can provide a good barometer of general engagement there is nothing so compelling as a measure of your own unique values. After all, you have made considerable efforts to establish what 'good performance' looks like in your specific organization, so not to measure progress against those specific values would be more than inconsistent.

Benchmarking for smaller organizations

It is an easy budget decision to buy into a global survey if you have tens of thousands of employees operating worldwide, as the cost per head will be minimal. As a smaller organization though, committing to a regular, detailed survey may be inappropriate from an absolute cost viewpoint. One way forward is to take part in one of the many 'Best Employers' surveys sponsored by a number of quality newspapers and media organizations. The benefit of answering the questions is a detailed report by value/issue of where you stand in relation to other organizations as a 'best employer'. Usually you are given a national ranking and then a per sector ranking. The key point of these surveys is not actually how high you score but what areas are identified for improvement. What you need from a benchmarking survey is pointers as to how to do better rather than a pat on the back for general past performance.

Construct your own survey

You should convene an internal engagement team and set about constructing your own survey against the values you have now adopted. The type of questions would cover personal development and talents, managerial style, work/life balance and perhaps communication. This could be interlaced with the new values of the organization to see if they are consistent. For example, if the survey question is about 'communicating with my line manager' the question could be: 'To what degree is my communication with my line manager consistent with our new value of openness and honesty: completely, very, ok, not very well, poorly?'

This exercise is not easy. Different members of your panel will have different views about what a good question is and whether you are 'leading the witness' and only asking questions for which you will get positive feedback. If this is your first ever in-depth survey you may well get somewhat negative views. People often use such opportunities as an excuse to unburden themselves of years of pent-up, workplace frustration. That's fine, as at least you are now listening. You can take heart that the second survey will be better, the third one even better, so there will be improvement going forward.

As for how long each survey should take, a general view would be that each response should take no longer than 15 minutes. Not only would this give the research organization some idea of the likely cost per sample size (they have to supply the telephone interviewers on a per hour basis) it reassures the sponsor that if they have to construct an online survey, the length of the interview or script draft is dictated by the 15-minute guideline.

'Burning platform' concept

It is unlikely that the senior team will have started the engagement process without some commercial triggers. Change can often be a result of reflection after a poor financial performance. Most employees will be pleased to know that action is under way to remedy performance and even more pleased when they realize that they are being asked to help, probably for the first time in this way. But beware the sceptics who publicly praise but privately criticize.

David Radford, Director, Market-Management at Allianz, the global German insurance group, with many years of experience in corporate communications, puts it like this:

> Usually there is a 'burning platform' of business challenges and probably poor results. This commercial imperative helps to galvanize support across the organization (for engagement initiatives). In my experience, the challenge in this regard is not those who speak up and raise objections, which can be addressed, but the 'cynics' who publicly make supportive noises, whilst privately criticizing.

Any local research organization can help you through this process, especially the architecture of the survey and its timing. When you brief them ensure that you specify what result you are looking for. You need to spell out in detail that you want to establish a starting, benchmark position for the values you are about to implement, not just an overall number. It may be that you want that number split between the centre, the manufacturing units, the site offices and perhaps subsidiaries, if you have any. What you are looking for is a credible basis for local action based on the values themselves and how they might be communicated.

Check your communication techniques

While you have the ear of your employees it would be efficient to check on the best way to communicate 'initiatives' with them going forward. It is a certainty that one complaint employees will have of any organization at any time is patchy internal communication. In truth there will always be gaps in communication, even in a small organization. Whether you have five employees or 5,000 no single medium will be perfect. If you send out a bulletin every day some employees will no doubt complain that you are overdoing it. But you should always check that the proposed ways to communicate are actually still relevant, especially if one of your engagement values is 'better communication'.

Less than 20 years ago there was no internet and no e-mail and team briefings, posters, memos and HR brochures were the favoured way to communicate new initiatives. Now, with intranets, private social networking sites, corporate Facebook, LinkedIn and Yammer, for example, as well as the traditional printed media, the content of any benchmarking survey would include questions about the most-effective/preferred method of communication for employees.

Getting 'engagement' with surveys

Much work and soul-searching will have been done to get to the point of briefing in an employee survey. You will want to get it distributed as soon as possible in order to see the results. The results will be highly anticipated by the development team. But one thing all researchers know is that response rates can be very low, depending on how the survey is marketed internally. Commercial research organizations know that consumers rarely complete sponsored surveys unless there is a benefit for them, hence the proliferation of prize draws and gift cards as incentives for completion. Employees are no exception as they are also consumers who know how to play the marketing game. It may be that you have to offer an inducement for employees to take part in the survey, such as discounted lunch vouchers, MP3 download credits or a prize draw for the latest electronics item.

You may need to vary the format of the survey depending on where the employees are sited and what access they may have to your various communication media. The obvious way to get high response rates is by e-mail on your intranet, provided the response does not take too long. But there may be job roles where people are unable to complete internal surveys during their normal work periods, in which case some sanctioned time needs to be set aside to enable as many employees as possible to complete the survey. If such surveys are going to be a regular occurrence it is worthwhile consulting with your steering group as to what might be appropriate in terms of when, how to do them and whether any token reward may be appropriate.

What response rates should you expect? Consumer product research response can be less than 1 per cent, but surveys of employees who are aware of the context and know that the process benefits them should be achieving 60 to 65 per cent completion. Response rates can be much enhanced by supporting such surveys with line manager introductions, face-to-face briefings and real-time feedback online about how many colleagues have completed the survey so far. Peer group pressure can be a wonderful thing.

Factor in other relevant measures

There are many other metrics that complete the engagement picture, so all the other 'normal' employee measurements should be retained as all data is useful when attempting to explain any anomalies. These metrics could be factors such as retention rates, absenteeism, diversity, training days, mentoring, number of freelances, pulse surveys, overheads vs sales, and perhaps new permanent hires. By itself each measure is only a symptom of how engaged employees are and the numbers will vary from group to group. As with all statistics it is the anomalies that indicate something systemic may be wrong – it is an example of management by exception. If nothing changes, there is no action to take, provided your engagement process is being carried through at all possible levels in the way that you want it to be conducted.

You may find it useful to create a 'dashboard' report for employee engagement so that reporting up and along the line is easily understood. This would be a single-page presentation with all the important metrics shown in a pictorial manner, usually with colour sections to show which issues need attention – a fuel gauge format is often the easiest design solution. In most cases a glance would be enough for anyone consulting the report to see that 'engagement' overall is steady but absenteeism is up, for example. The discussion can then focus on things that have changed rather than doggedly going through each metric only to find that not much has changed since last time.

Choice of questions

Engagement surveys are not the same as satisfaction surveys. Most satisfaction surveys are checking on what employees get out of their employment, such as benefits, working hours concessions, perks, wellbeing and other take-home items. This represents the benefits side of the employee contract, the employer giving to employees. Engagement surveys emphasize the contribution an employee makes to the business and how that contribution can be improved. So the questions will lean towards how well (or badly) employees *feel* they can contribute to the over-arching values of the business. Such issues as managerial style, teamwork, involvement, personal development and contributing ideas are all measures of positive engagement.

Robert Hogan, a psychologist at the University of Tulsa who has written extensively on the concept of 'happiness' at work, traced the development of employee surveys, which in the past have mostly been about workplace satisfaction. He charts how in earlier times it was enough to measure productivity as a guide to discovering whether employees were 'happy'. But happy for the employer was not necessarily happy for the employee, so other measures needed to be looked at. Measuring job involvement was next, which required psychological assessments of performance. Following this phase came 'organizational commitment to the job', which was then sub-divided into *affective commitment* (an employee's positive emotional attachment to the organization), *continuance* commitment (the degree to which the employee is tied to the business by economics and what would be lost by not being employed) and *normative* commitment (feelings of obligation towards colleagues and the organization's greater goals). Arguably these developments could be described as 'want to', 'have to' and 'ought to' in everyday life. It's not just about productivity anymore.

So at the heart of this development in measurement is the agreement that surveys now need to measure the emotional component of being at work and employees' feelings about the organization and their place within it. It has been a characteristic of hierarchy-based, numbers-driven organizations that emotional measures are seen as somewhat 'soft' and not worthy of senior attention. Nothing could be further from what is commercially effective. Engagement questions should focus on enthusiasm, flow and excitement at how employees can push the values process forward. Statements such as 'I feel excited', 'I find it easy to be focused', 'My line manager supports me', etc are the kind of content engagement surveys should be measuring.

Brand questions

You also need to cover questions about the employer brand and consumer brands in particular if you really want internal and external brand engagement. This additional area of the survey would not only raise the profile of brand perception but make an obvious link to the wider world of strategic brand engagement that is the interface with the consumer and the channel. These questions would mostly be about perceptions and trust in the employer brand and how compatible the employer brand is with the overall brand.

As before, the best way to get a useful measure for later comparison is to ask for levels of agreement for topics such as:

- *Values.* Are the new (ongoing) values compatible with the way the organization does business? Assess each value on its own merits. Would you add any other values? Are there any anomalies? Do people understand the values? Are they difficult to live up to? Are employees more trusting of the organization than before?

- *Customer brand.* Are the values consistent with consumer perceptions (provided they have been briefed on what they are)? Are there any mismatches? Are you able to keep the consumer brand promises? Do competitors do it better? How easy is it to establish your organization's difference with consumers? Have consumers noticed any difference?

- *Channel brand.* Is the channel aware of your new internal values? Does this give you a competitive advantage? Does the channel behave differently towards the organization now? Are commercial practices in the channel compatible with the new values? Do you get more commitment (not necessarily more orders) from the channel now? Has the channel noticed any difference?

- *Communication.* Do employees understand the new values? What could be done to make understanding better? Which media work best? Do employees need more or less communication? Are the results of the regular surveys useful/easy to interpret? Do new employees understand the new values/how do they find out about them? How well do the 'brand ambassadors' (see Chapter 8) do their job?

- *Recruitment.* Are the new values compatible with your recruitment and talent development strategies? Do your recruitment partners know enough about your values to help you recruit compatible people? Are you getting more internal applicants as a result of the engagement process? Do new recruits agree that other employees live the new brand?

The questions should be written in such a way that respondents do not feel obliged to be positive, otherwise you risk creating a false snapshot of opinion. Equally, negative answers should not be perceived by respondents as being in some way disloyal to the brand. If one of the main points about engagement is trust and honesty then this should be promoted in reassuring ways. But it is still an axiom in all market research that anonymity provides the best answers, so even if the survey is e-mailed and employees know the organization can trace who said what, there needs to be a protocol to reassure them that all answers are confidential and anonymous. Usually such surveys are conducted by external organizations via external websites with market research rules about confidentiality being highlighted at the top of each survey. In this way employees know they can respond openly and freely.

Consumer brand questions

The marketing function will be awash with consumer research, particularly in relation to your key markets, why consumers buy, the competition and current market trends. But almost all of this research will be outward facing and based on the perceived qualities of the product rather than the performance of employees. What strategic brand engagement requires is some data on what consumers think about your employees. This is highly relevant for organizations that have a direct link with their 'buyers' such as insurance, online products and government services. Using the same criteria outlined above you need to uncover what consumers think about how your employees deal with them, what values they think they exhibit and what improvements they might suggest to the process of dealing with consumers. Because most consumer products do not figure highly in their lives as a 'must-respond' issue, consumer research is likely to be by invitation, by telephone and in focus groups.

The objective of such research is to cross-check that the values being promoted internally are actually reaching the consumer in a significant way and to identify where it is not, in order to step up the engagement process. There is no point in having high levels of employee brand engagement if the consumer is treated as an outsider. Part of the package is that employees should be ambassadors for the brand and all touch points with the consumer are opportunities to demonstrate the new brand values.

Channel brand questions

It will be much harder to get responses from the channel than from employees as independent businesses are not obliged in any way to take part, so you may need to offer incentives of some kind for an effective response rate. In addition, you will probably get better response rates if the survey sponsor is hidden through anonymous researchers by asking questions about all the main manufacturers. Doing the survey this way avoids any skew that may be present if your organization is currently doing a specific promotion or there is some kind of product issue between you and the channel. This type of approach will reveal comparative scores with your competitors on emotional engagement with your brand, which would help to 'position' your relationship with distributors going forward and encourage more effort with specific distributors which in time would pay commercial dividends.

The channel research could also include your own employed sales or field force. This survey would be similar to the general employee version but with questions about salespeople as 'internal customers' and whether the brand values are in evidence when employed salespeople try to get internal services delivered, such as quotations, presentation materials, market information and contracts.

After the initial survey

Post initial-survey analysis

The internal team that put together the new values and the benchmarking engagement survey will be keen to analyse the initial findings and start implementing some change. But it is important to analyse the results of any survey carefully, taking into account any local, commercial or economic matters so as not to draw false conclusions.

For example, there is likely to be deeper understanding of the new values by those who work in the main executive/administrative office than in the outlying sites or in product distribution and it is very likely that scores will be uniformly lower. This is not to say that they are any less engaged but it may take time to get the key messages and behaviour change down to the grass roots of the organization. More frequent and more detailed communication may be required.

In any large organization there are bound to be rumours and speculation regarding mergers and acquisitions, often without any foundation. If an operating division has been underperforming and there is speculation in the business media about the ideal strategy, it is likely scores will be lower than predicted. Equally, if an organization has just been acquired its scores will be significantly different from the average engagement measures across the acquiring organization. It is a sensible idea to build in an additional 'sense-check' meeting with the research specialists before going public with any results as these factors may not be known to the researchers. The results may need to be adjusted to take account of ad hoc market factors, specific to certain employee groups.

Refining the engagement plan

The whole point of research is to find out something you did not know before and then change your organizational behaviour for the better. There may also be conflicting findings that would appear to contradict the general view, so it is quite possible that the next survey will need to be adjusted to explore in more detail some of the first, headline findings. It is quite common for some questions to be generally misunderstood or misinterpreted by certain sub-groups. These oddities can be cleaned up for the following survey to try to get more accurate results and better trend lines going forward.

Deal with the dark side

It is unlikely that the first engagement survey you do will be completely positive. In fact participants love to let you know their long-held beliefs about 'what is wrong with the organization' when they first get given the opportunity to voice an opinion. It is similar to an electorate voting for a minority party mid-term. When push comes to shove they still support the main party in government but from time to time they like to make sure it knows that it only exists with their loyal support, so please take notice of our views. Overall scores from the initial, benchmarking survey may be lower than you would expect.

There may even be parts of the organization or issues that are shockingly poor in terms of positive feedback. This may be the result of political issues within the organization, local management style or even the fear that the survey is simply a prelude to major reorganization and redundancies. If there are misunderstandings or misinterpretations, executive action may need to be taken to explore these issues quickly or correct them through the usual communication channels before the rumour mill starts.

On a more positive note the survey may throw up areas of improvement that could be the subject of an immediate, operational working party. Few organizations regularly survey the opinions of the channel, for example. The survey may uncover process issues to do with ordering new stock or dealing with financial reporting. It may be that the organization was unaware that the issue was a major concern to the distributor and may well be the underlying reason why that distributor was not 'fully engaged' with your organization in recent months or years.

Making 'transformational' changes both in practical terms and in terms of attitudes are the instant wins from an improved engagement process, only made possible through knowing what people think and, more important, how they feel about your organization. One of those feelings may well be curiosity: having asked very searching and detailed questions about engagement, is the enterprise going to do anything about what it has discovered? One of the most damaging exercises any organization can undertake is to conduct an unusual and extensive survey of its employees and business partners with no obvious result. At the very least the findings need to be communicated to those who took part, even if no action follows. So communicating the results is the next key task, and this is explored in the next chapter.

Marketing brand engagement internally

07

We call it employer brand: how a business builds and packages its identity, from its origins and values, what it promises to deliver, to emotionally connect employees so that they in turn deliver what the business promises to customers. **(SARTAIN AND SCHUMANN, 2006)**

Following the benchmarking survey and having made any tweaks to the brand values as a result of the initial feedback it is time to plan and communicate the new brand engagement values, initially to employees. Much has changed since the adoption of the internet (say post-1995) when it comes to employee communication. The use of intranets and closed group online communications deserves a book in itself, possibly many. You will find some useful online strategies in Chapter 10 on 'social networking' as applied to brand engagement.

In time-honoured tradition marketing a brand to any audience includes four main elements and communicating with employees is no exception. The four issues to consider are product (what the values actually are), price (the cost of internal communication in this instance), promotion (how to get attention for the proposition) and place (the distribution of the various employee audiences).

Some basics about corporate communication

There is a well-known story in marketing circles about brand misinterpretation. A Scottish whisky distiller wanted to expand into Europe and decided it would test its product in Germany, one of Europe's biggest markets for whisky. It had commissioned a graphic artist to create an illustration of a Scottish stag on a mountain crag with swirling mists and rain clouds to be reproduced on the label. It was so taken with the quality of the illustration that it decided to call the product 'Scotch Mist'. But when it piloted the product in Germany, sales were very disappointing. It was only later that it realized that *mist* is the German word for dung. The image suggested to German consumers that the whisky was a natural by-product of the stag on the label.

FIGURE 7.1   Communication is a two-way process

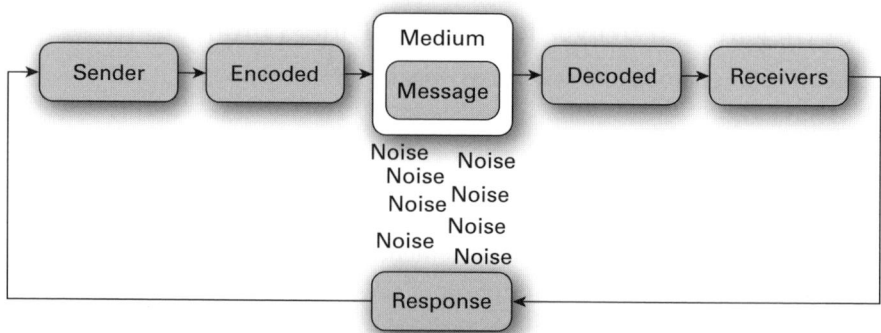

SOURCE: Motivation Diploma course notes, Institute of Promotional Marketing, UK, 2012

It seems obvious to point out that communication is a two-way process but in many instances enterprises behave as if it is just one-way. Top-down pronouncements are often the default mechanism for traditional organizations with little thought given to feedback or even consulting with their various audiences before 'policy decisions' are imposed on the unfortunate employee groups. Organizational communication within the context of strategic brand engagement should always be two-way with the emphasis on feedback; see Figure 7.1. Let's walk through this in detail:

- The sender always has an implied authority (or lack of it) so any messages will be perceived in the context of who sent it. This is important when establishing tone of voice to the various audiences. In many instances the 'obvious' sender from an HR perspective may not be the obvious sender with authority when viewed by functional areas or site operations. So when a message about engagement needs to be sent you need to consider whether one sender is appropriate or whether it requires several senders with slightly different content and tone of voice to different employee groups.

- The basic message needs to be encoded to suit the audience. The encoding not only includes the basic information but the style or even creative treatment of the message. A message about engagement to functional heads may include figures, reports, executive agreements and timings, with a fairly flat, matter-of-fact tone. The same message to junior staff may well include pictorial elements and be upbeat in its approach with little mention of numbers or strategy. Whichever encoding technique is chosen the sender needs to be very clear what he or she wants to happen as a result of the message being received. It is surprising how many organizational messages are sent that appear to have no obvious response requirement. The result, of course, is that the message is not interpreted as intended and nothing happens. With no feedback mechanism there is no opportunity for the sender to find out whether everyone agrees with the message or whether they are quietly angry about what has just been suggested.

- The effect on engagement will change depending on the medium chosen. E-mails are the obvious first choice for employee communication, simply because they are easy and inexpensive to send. But ease of use does not always mean effective. For some employee groups you may need to present face-to-face first, as in a team briefing, supported by a detailed e-mail later on. It could be that some promotional posters in the working environment would be appropriate or a CEO video on the intranet to provide the background to the more specific communication. It may even be that an all-managers conference needs to be held to share the message with them first before it gets distributed to their teams.

- Noise is a significant factor in employee disengagement. 'Noise' is the technical term for any kind of message interference such as conflicting instructions, another important message at the same time, bigger issues that overshadow your message, negative interpretation by line managers and so on. When you send your message, have you made a careful check on 'noise' with regard to timing and tone of voice?

- When employees decode your message what parts are they likely to misinterpret, misunderstand or misconstrue? Is your language appropriate to your audience? It is all too easy to slip into jargon if you are developing a major engagement initiative, borrowing technical phrases from the consultants when drilling down into the nuances of employee behaviour. But when the message goes out, it is a good discipline to ask someone not involved with the project to sense-check it. The financial services industry is still prone to lazy use of language and some of the poor brand perception of that sector can be explained by using technical jargon that means nothing to most consumers, and often their own employees.

- When the receivers finally get the message are you able to check what they think it means and are there any points that you did not get across? Feedback mechanisms are an important part of any communications plan. This could be a pilot test, a trial with one section of the audience, a pre-announcement managers' briefing, formal research feedback or even ad hoc comments, post-announcement, using your corporate Facebook or a closed blog.

Like brand reputations, new engagement initiatives can quickly become disengagement if attention is not given to the basics of good organizational communications. All the planning will be of no use if the audiences you want to engage with decide that, for any of the reasons above, they do not want to engage with you.

Recruit widely for the engagement team

Strategic brand engagement requires a cross-functional team. It is obvious that HR has a role, but communication is stock in trade for marketing people so their skills need to be represented on that team as well. They can provide the consumer interface so that the team does not do something that would be at odds with consumer perceptions of the brand values. You also need to have representation from the main engagement targets within the organization, such as manufacturing, warehousing, administration and sales.

Externally you will need someone from the channel to represent their views. In practical terms this is likely to be someone from your employed field team who knows the channel partners from day-to-day experience; he or she will be able to provide informed feedback on how to communicate with them.

Ideally steering groups should be as small as possible to avoid long, drawn-out meetings and the inevitable diary clashes. If you have a multi-site organization this may be a good opportunity to use Skype or other online meeting devices to keep both costs and time down as most people will have their main job to do as well as being involved with a new engagement project.

Packaging the brand values

In Chapter 4 we explored the idea that the master brand may have sub-brands and that the consumer brand may not correlate completely with the employer brand. To an automobile manufacturer it seems obvious that each model has a different personality in promotional terms, as they are aimed at different segments of the market. But the master brand is the same across all products. This could be manifested, for example, by the master brand promise of quality and reliability. The employer brand services all types of customer so their values are derived from the master brand and interpreted internally as process or transactional values. There are many diagrams to illustrate how the various elements interact but they all share the same broad features; see Figure 7.2.

FIGURE 7.2　Branding model

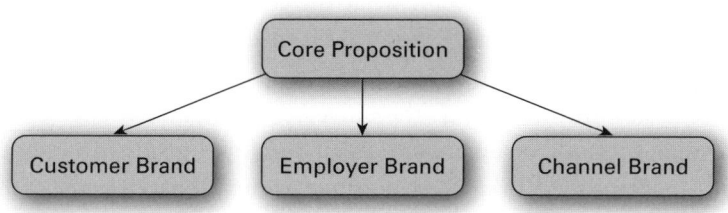

The core proposition is the over-arching strategic brand – a collection of reliable values – that is unique to the organization and provides a starting point and a focus for definitions of what the organization is all about. The customer brand is a simple, mass media translation of the core proposition expressed in language the consumer can respond to. In many cases it may be as simple as a logo in the bottom corner of the advertisement to show who the manufacturer is. In other cases it may include a strapline that expresses a simple value – 'We try harder' – that can be understood across all products. In addition there will be product statements that underpin why the consumer should buy that particular brand within that market.

The employer brand strapline could be the same as the core proposition to keep things simple and aligned, or it could be different. It can be argued that some shoe-horning often goes on here because the consumer wants slightly different things from the brand promise. The customer wants good value for money and reliability whereas the employee wants personal development and job security. So, for some organizations there may be merit in having another strapline that is derived from the benefits of being in the organization as an employee, how the employer differs from other similar employers or a unique value/reason to work there. Phrases such as 'Believe in Better' or 'Working Together' could be a natural complement to straplines such as 'Better Made' or 'We're with you', respectively. The main point is that if a separate employer brand strapline is chosen it needs to align very strongly with the core proposition otherwise, in marketing speak, brand integrity is compromised and employees begin to wonder why the message internally is potentially at odds with the message to the outside world.

Within the channel it is likely that you will want to use the core proposition, as this will be familiar from general brand promotion, and adapt the values that derive to the commercial supplier/manufacturer relationship. If, for example the core proposition is 'Better by far' the service levels and deal-making need to take into account what the competition is doing and what processes the organization goes through to ensure a 'better by far' result as perceived by the channel. To some extent the channel engagement proposition is the easiest of the three as the universe of potentially engaged people is often smaller than consumers and most employee groups so adaptations are more easily agreed than for the other groups. The channel should be seen in communication terms as a special sub-group of what consumers see and experience. The consumer experience should be replicated within the channel and the same customer process values should be implemented to offer a similar brand experience.

International aspects

There has been much discussion in recent years about the 'glocalization' of brands and services. Thinking global but acting local is not easily done, however. In marketing terms the less targeted the audience, the blander and less relevant the communication will be for each segment of the audience. We have all come across the phenomenon of 'airport ads' where a well-known local brand becomes almost unrecognizable when presented to an international audience with differing perceptions of what the advertiser stands for. Inevitably the communication will catch no-one's attention if it is too broad.

The same is true of an employer brand. A brand statement with no regard to local employer groups will be perceived as wallpaper if it is always stripped down to its absolute essentials. One way around this puzzle is to retain a headline employer brand logo but then reposition the components to be relevant to local employee groups using local images and design styles. The logo then becomes the shortcut for all the attached values.

CASE STUDY Coca-Cola

Coca-Cola is one of the world's most recognizable consumer brands and the trademark (the logo) does a good job in promoting a product promise with no words being necessary. It has 40 derived brands enjoyed by 170 million consumers annually. Chinese children who read no English still recognize the image as 'Coca-Cola', a soft drink with a predictable but unique taste.

In 2012 Coca-Cola Enterprises presented details of its employer brand journey called 'Building Capability' for Northern Europe, a cross-border initiative to recruit more employees. It determined that its employer brand for recruitment purposes needed to be authentic, different and relevant to its many local employee audiences. It chose the theme 'Thirst for First' and presented its three values in a comic book style using photographic images of real people as the medium. The images were relayed through various online media as well as in the recruitment press.

Although this was purely a recruitment tool it is a good example of thinking through the employer brand and how it is perceived by potential employees as well as consumers. The principles of echoing engagement values in its external advertising for new employees is a good example of strategic brand engagement, supporting the brand at all touch points, not just at the commercial transaction level.

The cost of communication

So, having carefully considered the 'product' (what employer's values to communicate) with sensitivity towards how the messages are going to be perceived, we need to look at the relative costs of engagement communication – the 'price'.

The skill of marketing communications is not just how the message looks but in the management of scarce resources to get the most effective result. It's easy to get a message across when money is no problem, but in all marketing situations, media cost is the key issue in the success or failure of any communications campaign. There's no point in having a great idea if not enough people or even the right people get to know about it.

There are many paid-for and 'free' media that could be used to disseminate the engagement plan to your own employees and the channel. Of course, no media are completely without cost. An intranet will already exist as a tool for internal communications but most intranets are relatively static: they display fixed information that changes on a regular basis in the same way that magazines have new printed issues. The social networking element may be available but you would need to visit that page to see what has changed, but it may look the same as the day before. To promote a new message some design/copywriting and coding resource will be needed to ensure the main points of the initial research are well-communicated on the home page with perhaps a new link to the new information. There may be several variants depending on which subsidiary needs what data. For a small organization this is straightforward, but for a multi-site enterprise one message for all may not be the answer. So additional 'creative' expense needs to be allowed for in order to think through who should receive what and how much should be said.

The same cost argument applies to social networking. Many large organizations use various forms of the corporate Facebook model but very few are actively updated and used to their full potential. The answer is to allocate resources to professional, external social networkers who can roam the system, encouraging those with poor profiles to update them and join various chat groups, but also to provoke conversation and dialogue through collaboration groups and forums. There is a cost attached to this activity, which is normally time-based. A good system will use employees to do most of this job but initially and at strategic moments such 'informal' activity needs to be directed from outside in much the same way as a recruitment specialist will produce more candidates by external activity rather than relying on the good will of salaried employees to produce referrals.

CASE STUDY   Driving traffic to the intranet

One example of the need to drive employees to internal sites comes from the construction industry. A major global engineering organization had been acquiring subsidiaries at a frenetic rate in recent years and as a result had built up a network of intranet sites of varying degrees of quality and usefulness. English was just one of many languages being used. Despite the acquisitions it was felt that subsidiaries were still guilty of silo thinking and did not share expertise and contacts for the benefit of the overall organization to reap the rewards of being one corporate entity. Fingers were pointed at the plethora of intranets. A plan was devised to build a centralized intranet, which took many months. But the people issue remained. Employees still hankered after their local sites and rarely visited the main site. An incentive strategy was devised to encourage employees to share information and offer updated profiles to the main site in return for local rewards of gift cards. In effect it was a points-mean-prizes scheme. The amounts were not large but enough to force a change of habit. At the same time local sites were gradually closed down leaving employees with no option but to use the central site for expertise exchange. It also gave the organization the opportunity to debate what it really needed from an intranet and what benefits closer cooperation could bring. Familiarity with social networking models and techniques helped it build a site that appealed to a younger generation and made it more comfortable with sharing ideas than was the case prior to the creation of the central site and the closing down of the local sites.

Paid-for media

There should be a budget for off-line promotional items that relay the main values, including printed posters, semi-permanent wall graphics, notice-board updates, hanging banners (open-plan offices), notepads, desk stickers, low-cost giveaways, printed guidelines, briefing notes for new recruits, team briefing support, printed newsletters and video briefings, to name but a few. Although these items are a small part of the overall project budget they play a significant role in the ongoing visibility of the scheme once the impact of the live briefings and manager workshops has faded.

Some projects benefit from 'wallpaper change', which means that various aspects of the initiative could be promoted on a rolling basis with new features to raise employee awareness each quarter, say. Schneider Electric, the French power conglomerate, changes its employer brand every three years to reflect the updated business strategy. The current employer brand is called 'Connect' which took the place of 'One' that covered the period 2010–13. All marketers know that the initial launch is just the start and that to get the messages truly embedded, promotion to any audience should be ongoing.

As the time for follow-up surveys and measures comes onto the horizon, any misunderstandings or revised interpretations from the employee or consumer research could be incorporated into the communications plan. It may be that one of the values, such as 'great service' may not be perceived by customers as having improved at all. In that case the internal messages need to be tweaked to concentrate on that failing measure, rather than simply repeating the general messages.

Meetings/briefings and ROI

Much has been written and commented in recent years about the return on investment (ROI) from meetings, conferences and events. This is relatively straightforward for public exhibitions and B2B events where actual sales or market share can be easily deduced as the financial justification for invest-ing in them. The pioneering work of Dr Elling Hamso and the ROI Institute is well worth consulting to see how it should be done for conferences and events (visit **www.eventroi.org** to learn more). The Event ROI Institute was founded in 2005 as a partnership of European consultants dedicated to improving the value of meetings and events. It offers training courses and in-house training and consultancy services, seeking better ways to maximize value and reduce costs. The Event ROI Institute has an exclusive partnership agreement with Jack Phillips, the world-renowned expert on accountability, measurement, and evaluation, and ROI Institute Inc for the meetings and events industry in Europe.

Employee conferences can be difficult to justify

Strategic employee meetings are less obvious to account for. To hold an internal meeting on site for, say, three hours would require a complicated financial calculation based on the total employee remuneration of attendees, lost productivity, cost of follow-up activities and a somewhat subjective assessment of what commercial benefits would ensue from employees being better informed rather than not being informed face-to-face. Sometimes you just have to take a leap of faith and believe that taking a few hours of employee time to refocus them on a new engagement approach would be inherently beneficial and is already factored into the cost of their employment.

External events are more easily examined. There will be a cost for the venue, the food and beverage, transport, potential overnight accommodation, external speakers, if any, and any external logistics management. You may also wish to factor in the 'time out of the office' if it is a significant cost. In this scenario you will need to make a decision as to whether the new message is so fundamental to the future direction of the business that it needs to be done in an impactful way that they will remember it – which probably means an external event.

Another approach could be that team leaders and management are briefed off site so that confidential feedback can be obtained in a relaxed environment, with the team briefings happening on site to minimize both the cost and disruption to the organization's daily life. Such meetings tend to be relatively unusual and so it should be possible to measure changed perceptions and performance from doing it, which in itself may well be worth paying for. As Marshall McLuhan, the Canadian communications theorist, once famously stated: 'the medium is the message'. The very fact that people are being taken out of their normal working environment gives the message more credence and memorability than if it were communicated in a more traditional, cascaded manner in the office.

New engagement strategies are not routine news

The key message about strategic brand engagement costs is that the task cannot be done using the normal parameters of employee communication.

A major change of direction in thinking and re-evaluation of how you want all your employees to behave in future is not like sending out a superannuation flyer. The process of communicating at launch, the ongoing survey results and the regular promotions all stack up costs in the same way that a consumer advertising campaign accumulates. The engagement budget needs to reflect this, otherwise all your thinking and plans for change will not flourish and bear fruit in terms of changed employee attitudes. It may be perceived as yet another HR 'programme' that is not reinforced and therefore fades away in time due to lack of adequate repetition and follow-through.

Promoting employee engagement

Assuming the costs of promotion, even internally, have been allowed for, you now need to actually do something different. Internal promotion is not easy because all employees have a 'day-job' and, if well-directed, they will be focused on delivering what they do to the best of their abilities for customers rather than sitting around waiting for your next message about brand engagement. You need to be intrusive without being irrelevant in much the same way that consumer advertising and promotion works.

The disciplines of running a marketing campaign apply equally to employee brand marketing. The 'product' may be well-known to your audiences and employees will be aware of the main new elements. But once the novelty of the launch messages have worn off, you need to consider how to revive interest in a topic most employees will now see as 'old news'. The best way to do this is to pre-plan a campaign of sub-messages that underpin the employer brand over time, with defined activities linked to those specific messages.

An annual campaign

Typically you could divide the year up into four cycles, following the sales pattern of the year, if there is one, and promote engagement about one or more of the key values. The periods do not have to be even. It may suit your organization to run them for, say, two months, four months, four months, then two months, for example. If you are part of a very large organization it may be more practical to refresh the brand every six months to give employees time to hear the new message, respond to it and embed it fully into their everyday working lives.

Tactical campaigns example

Let's walk through an example. A large manufacturing organization has implemented a new employer brand, after much research and soul-searching. The four new employer brand elements are respect, friendliness, challenge and reliability. The year would be split up into suitable time periods where these four elements would be explored promotionally through the intranet and other employee media. The first tactical campaign would feature examples of 'respect' asking employees to share examples on the intranet of how 'respect' is visible in the organization with perhaps small, token rewards for the best examples. It could be promoted using Aretha Franklin's 'Respect' YouTube clip to get attention, if this suits your employee profile.

The second period campaign could be themed 'You need friends...' with online quizzes to name popular music artists who have released songs with 'friends' in the title and maybe a competition for employees to submit their own song performed by a group of friends, to be judged online by their peers. The winning 'team of friends' wins tickets to a pop/rock concert of their choice. The point about such activities is that they lift the message from being something theoretically strategic to something fun and active that employees can participate in and enjoy. At the same time everyone is getting the message that 'friendliness' is a key organizational value that can be applied in a number of ways, and that if this approach works with colleagues it can also work with business partners in the channel and ultimately with consumers in terms of underpinning the organization's master brand values.

Peer group recognition schemes

Rather than re-think new promotions every quarter many organizations support their employer brand with formal recognition schemes that use the core employer brand values as the mechanism to recognize and reward employee actions. Known as 'peer group recognition programmes' they provide a formal system for employees at all levels to 'vote' for other employees who demonstrate the new core values. Typically each month all employees are given a small number of nominations which they can make for 'values activity', recording their votes via a specific micro site on the organizational intranet. These votes have supporting documentation or comments attached which are then vetted by their line supervisor, all online, and recognition by way of a congratulations message is sent directly to the employee being recognized. Each nomination carries a points or credits value and token awards in the form of online credits or gift cards may be given.

The same system can apply to teams by nominating a specific team that has demonstrated one or more of the core values. At the end of the period or year the very best/most often recognized employees or teams of employees may be invited for a more formal ceremony, hosted by senior executives, such as a dinner or an awards night. National prizes, such as family holidays may be awarded for the very best examples of demonstrating core employee brand values, with publicity distributed about the winners and relevant highlighted examples. It is classic testimonial marketing ('Look what I did and what I got... and you could be like me').

CASE STUDY   Chevron brings out the best

Chevron Chemical has had recognition programmes for employees for many years. One of them, 'Bringing out the Best', came about as a result of employee research, which showed that they felt the old scheme relied too much on supervisor nominations and as a result less than 50 per cent of employees actively participated. The revised programme excluded the supervisory layer completely and all nominations were made peer-to-peer for the first time; this had an additional benefit of reducing the amount of central administration required. There was some online vetting to check the authenticity of some submissions and frivolous nominations were excluded.

Employees could now recognize any examples of 'best practice' they felt appropriate at any time, following simple core value guidelines. Each nomination granted to the nominee a fixed 'thank you' retail voucher but to keep the quality of nominations high, they could only nominate up to six colleagues per year. There was no limit on the nominations each employee could receive or on who could nominate whom – a VP could nominate the mailroom operative if they wanted.

In the first year of this revised scheme 70 per cent of employees gave out three or more nominations and over 90 per cent of the workforce considered the programme to be good or very good in recognizing outstanding workplace performance. The 'instant' feature of the scheme whereby employees could be recognized at any time, not just when the supervisors had had their decision meeting, was regarded as a major step forward in making the initiative come alive as a relevant part of the new employer brand.

It is clear that revising the name of the programme and tweaking the rules helped to raise its profile amongst employees in the same way that old products are revived in the consumer environment by new designs and new features. Engagement needs to be refreshed from time to time like any other product to get continued commitment.

'Eureka' – ideas/suggestion schemes

An alternative way to promote an engagement initiative is to repurpose your suggestions or ideas scheme. Suggestion schemes have been around a long time in large organizations but arguably they faded into the background in recent years as they were seen as being old-fashioned and of limited commercial use. Now this has changed with the advent of the intranet. The long and often tedious task of sifting through 'new ideas' manually and holding time-consuming assessment meetings has been much improved by online submissions, evaluations and responses by the necessary steering groups and vetting procedures. Traditionally ideas schemes have concentrated on cost savings and revenue generation alone.

CASE STUDY   Siemens, Congleton: suggestion scheme

The Siemens plant in Congleton, UK employs 400 people and generates over 4,000 suggestions a year with around 3,000 of those implemented, generating savings of almost £1 million a year. Significantly the scheme has no paperwork, just an intranet application with each manager evaluating the ideas. When an idea is accepted, recognition is in the form of gift cards. The Siemens concept is to give token recognition on acceptance rather than larger amounts after the idea has been implemented. A key factor in the scheme's success is the publication of department league tables, with further departmental awards giving the managers an incentive to accept good ideas rather than focusing on their implementation.

(I am grateful to Ideas UK for a good example of an effective ideas scheme without paper.)

Taking the lead from organizational core values, an ideas programme could be based on ideas which stem from the *new values* and as such they 'qualify' for points and rewards. Using the example above credits could be given for suggesting ways to create 'respect' in the workplace such as replying to internal e-mails within 48 hours or unblocking meeting rooms if there is an unexpected cancellation. There is no reason why the cost-savings/revenue generation element could not remain, but the main purpose of the revised scheme would be to support the new engagement values at a practical level that most employees could relate to and participate in.

Tell employees about sector surveys

Most employees are keenly aware who their commercial rivals are within their sector. Another way to focus attention on everyday changes in behaviour is to publish the regular sector surveys on employee engagement. They often show same-sector organizations in rank order format so that employees can see where they stand in their particular market. Sometimes it is possible to compare specific measures if the organization has subscribed to a general survey such as 'customer satisfaction' or 'speed of query response'. Even if that level of detail is not available, simply knowing that your organization is in the top quartile for engagement adds an external element of competition and encouragement to maintain or improve market position. Some supervisors use the regular report as a talking point at team briefings to explore how things could be improved, and so enthusiasm for the programme is revived with minimal expenditure.

A further aspect of market surveys could be using some media issue as a 'call to action'. Regaining the support of ordinary financial consumers after the much publicized loss of trust in banks and investment institutions on both sides of the Atlantic seems like a very difficult hill to climb. Surveys that show how 'bad' financial customer service is could be turned to advantage by isolating which elements of the process are annoying consumers the most (applications taking too long to process?) and working out how to improve them as part of an engagement initiative.

Even if your engagement programme is working well, it will need new content all the time to keep the issues fresh in the minds of employees. High profile media campaigns and news stories about your industry sector are useful sources of material to galvanize employees into renewed action for improvement.

Places of engagement

The final element of the marketing jigsaw is always the place(s) or distribution of the message. In external marketing this normally means the channels through which you sell your products. For an employee engagement initiative 'place' could be seen as the various audiences you need to send the message out to. For a small organization working from one site, knowing who to share the message with is not usually an issue, but multi-site and international organizations face particular challenges when you want to market your engagement programme to more than one location.

Cascades and Chinese Whispers

Most of us are familiar with the game Chinese Whispers where the instigator whispers a message in the next person's ear with the instruction not to ask for clarification, but simply to repeat what they thought they heard. After a few exchanges it is clear that the message has been distorted, often with hilarious consequences. This is amusing at home but not so comical in an organizational context when trying to align employees with your values.

The further away from the middle employees are, the more likely that corporate messages will be misunderstood and distorted. So 'distribution' is all about recognizing this social phenomenon and taking steps to minimize the misunderstanding. In practical terms a plan should be drawn up to identify how many sub-groups there are in the employee universe and which groups should be treated the same or differently. In a single-site situation there could be five to 10 sub-groups for a medium-size organization. For each group the distribution plan should then determine the relevant stages for communication – maybe a leadership e-mail and video, followed by manager briefings, followed by small team briefings, followed by feedback, followed by feedback from the feedback.

In a multi-site situation it may be that specific divisions get the message first... or last, for various operational reasons, so some planning needs to be undertaken to work out who hears what and when. It may be that the same senior people need to go on a road show to all sites to deliver the message in person, so there will be an inevitable time lag between the first show and the last. Does this matter in the context of your organization? If it does, what's your plan? If the roll-out of the message takes several weeks, would this interfere with any operational or process issues in the organization?

Is there a good period and a not-so-good period to be communicating this message, such as around public holiday periods or crucial commercial dates for the organization?

In an international context, should the message be distributed to all regions simultaneously or should it be a stepped launch? Should it start 'at home' or should it be piloted on the other side of the world? Do you need to consider whether the launch plan media are as appropriate in say, India as they are in Indiana? Numbers of employees make a difference: a plan to disseminate information to 1,000 employees in a Town Hall meeting is very different when seen in the context of a European 'sales office' that only has 20 people.

Accept the 80/20 rule and move on

When you have worked through your four Ps – product, promotion, price and place (distribution) and possibly packaging if appropriate – for your new engagement programme, you may be forgiven for asking what, with such meticulous planning, could possibly go wrong? The answer is, of course, the human factor. However well everything is prepared there will be some employees who will be psychologically disinclined to participate, or be planning to leave the organization, or will not like the changes or even feel that this new way of dealing with workplace relationships is not for them.

We know from engagement statistics that less than 50 per cent engagement causes organizational drag – it becomes less efficient than it could be – and that anything above 80 per cent engagement is exceptional employee support for similar programmes. So unlike a religion, you should never expect 100 per cent alignment to the cause: 80 per cent is good enough and much better than most.

The fifth 'P' is participation or people

Marketing folk have argued for many years about other 'P' words that take the marketing concept further. We just added 'P for packaging' above, for example. There are probably seven or eight Ps now if you care to look hard enough. But one important additional P to consider for an employee engagement marketing plan is certainly P for participation. New media marketer Chris Heuer coined the phrase 'participation is marketing' in 2005 in one of his blogging pieces, which can still be viewed on Chris Heuer's

Insytes site at **www.chrisheuer.com**. He was talking about the fact that it is no longer acceptable in our information-rich world simply to promote or push new products – you have to get involved with your 'community' and give something back. This leads on to the difficult topic of social media and how employees can participate in the brand online without triggering lawsuits and other public damage to the brand. (There is more on this topic in Chapter 10 because social media now affect all methods of engagement and continue to be a challenge to get right.)

Meanwhile, what about the sales people and the channel? In many organizations the sales team and the independent distribution channels are largely left to their own devices – nobody understands how difficult our job is, they say, so let us sort it out. The problem is that when it comes to market share sometimes the rules get bent out of shape in the pursuit of targets. The first casualty is usually the brand and its values. The next chapter deals with those who promote your products but who may be employed by someone else or not employed by anyone. They also need to be engaged with your brand.

Ambassadorship and advocacy: taking the employer brand into the channel

08

> *Organizations should actively nurture a culture of partner engagement so that, like employees and customers, channel partners become emotionally engaged and are more likely to take an active interest in the organization's success.*
>
> **(CONYNGHAM PERFORMANCE GROUP, MAY 2012)**

It should be clear now that aligning positive performance with shared employee values not only makes for a happier and more stable workplace but creates better financial performance. The atmosphere of trust that is characteristic of well-engaged organizations can only ever have good outcomes. So, it is logical that it would be beneficial to extend that engagement programme to other commercial partners who have close links to your organization. They may not be fully employed or controlled by you as employees but your success largely depends on their success. They are your network of distributors, collaborators and even volunteers.

But there could be a number of types of distributor/partner, so it is important to draw some distinctions because each of these groups is somewhat

FIGURE 8.1 Channel engagement model

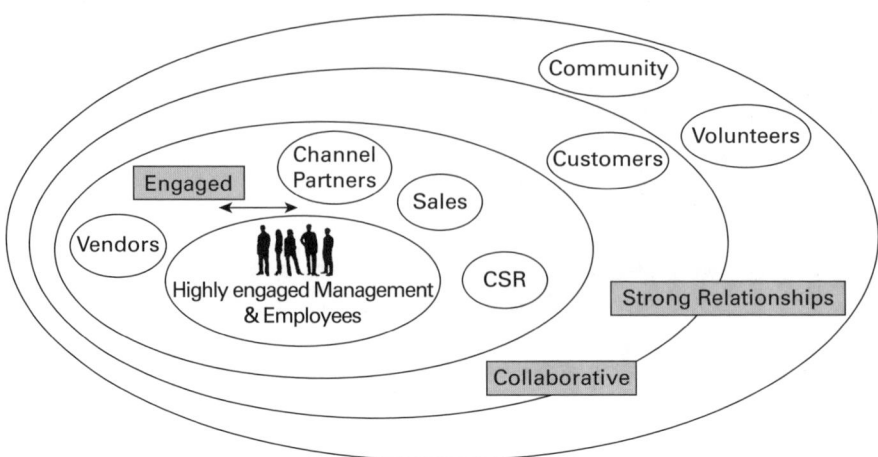

SOURCE: Enterprise Engagement Alliance/Conyngham Performance Group, 2012

removed from the organization's hub; see Figure 8.1. The key point of difference is that they are not directly controlled by the organization and often, other than goodwill, they have no reason to be loyal if other priorities take precedence. Any strategic engagement plan needs to take into account their degrees of separation from the fully-employed group. Closest to your organization are your own employed sales, zone or regional field teams. Next come your channel partners who sell on your behalf to end-users, both business and retail, but who have their own culture. Then there are vendors who sell to your organization. It is also quite possible to have collaborative links with customer groups in terms of bulk purchases or promotional deals. At the outer edge are charitable links and volunteer groups who you may work with for no commercial gain but with whom you have shared values about how the world could be made a better place – sponsored healthcare facilities or environmental projects, for example. Normally these groups would be part of a CSR (Corporate Social Responsibility) initiative. But they still need to be aligned with your brand values.

In short there are three main areas of influence that any engagement VP needs to consider within the strategic brand engagement plan: your employed sales or field force, your channel partners and your retailer partners. Useful as your charity volunteers are, your commercial partners are probably the most important groups with whom you need to be aligned and engaged in a significant and formal way.

Employed sales forces

The internet has probably done away with the need for very large sales teams of representatives in most of the developed world as it has made information exchange so much easier. Developments in the online meetings industry and Skype have also meant that there is less need for personal representation when it is just a question of data and facts rather than persuasion. With information, even about complicated products and services, now being readily available 24/7 there is a much smaller need for the show-and-tell style of channel sales representative who used to be the dominant alternative to retail sales. That said, in a number of high-margin complex sales story markets there is still a need for employed representation, such as pharmaceuticals or financial services where the 'customers' may well be professional buyers on behalf of other consumers or have such complex needs that only a bespoke service will do. Automotive still falls into this category due to the complexity of the product, the high unit cost and the frequent need for financial support when purchasing a car.

Professional services such as medical or legal skills may well be the exception, although even within these markets there is a certain amount of commoditization. Property may be another 'special case' where the internet has not yet totally taken over the sales process.

Keep salespeople in the brand loop

The brand engagement issue here is the fact that some salespeople are not 'in the office' for most of the working day and so touch points with the values of your organization may be few and far between. It is not easy to feel fully engaged with your employer if you work from home and your only true engagement is the finance area or the annual convention, if there is one. Employed salespeople may feel more allegiance to their loyal customers than the organization, especially if they work remotely or in the field.

It is important to involve the employed sales team in the formulation of the brand values as they will be acutely aware of the organization's failings 'out there in the real world'. They will have first-hand experience of trying to support central initiatives that may seem perfectly sound when viewed internally but not so effective when business partners try to implement the new process or system. This is particularly true of financial reporting systems. In addition they will be much closer to the channel or the consumer in terms of authentic delivery of the brand and will be more critical of some of the glib phrases that tend to be produced from within the organization in terms of touch points, trust and reliability. For example it is easy to say that one of your engagement values is 'to treat the customer as king'. But if, when face-to-face with a real customer or a distributor, salespeople cannot access customer records in a reliable way the service is unlikely to be truly 'regal'. The fact that office-based employees are never in this situation means that providing reliable data links does not tend to be a 'values priority' in the ongoing discussions about brand engagement.

When the new values are launched and teams are trying to understand how to translate the values into their everyday working life, the sales team needs to invent its own engagement applications that apply to prospecting, customer presentations, follow-up procedures and contract specification/ negotiation. Sales interface examples will be completely different from internal administration staff processes. The engagement plan needs to reflect this and be fully joined up so that salespeople do not become detached from the process.

Sales incentive programmes

One important cross-check to make is the structure and promotion of any existing employee sales incentive programmes. It is common for KPI (key performance indicator) incentives and non-cash incentives to reward specific sales activities... but are they in line with the new engagement values? A balanced scorecard approach is the safe way to go as this normally covers all the main things you want to see in salespeople's performance, rather than just the numbers they produce. But take care that, say, leads generation does not become the tail that wags the dog and your engagement brand value of 'providing the best service' does not become second best because they are all concentrating on leads and appointments, instead of supporting core values, to win the incentive prizes on offer.

Incentive travel as an engagement tool

One UK life insurance sales organization signed up to values of 'compliance with best industry practice codes of conduct' and yet ran a sales-based incentive trip to Las Vegas. It was felt after the trip that spending policy-holders' money on an all-expenses-paid holiday for just a tiny proportion of the sales team was in breach of its new brand engagement values. The following year, it still ran a convention but this time it was a domestic event that turned out to be equally enjoyable but nowhere near as expensive and high profile. Qualification was based on a mixed set of core values compliance and pre-agreed KPIs rather than sales. It also added a master class on sales skills, even though it was a leisure event, to bring it back into line with trying to service the customer better.

It is fair to say in Europe that incentive travel as the default incentive mechanism for above-average employed sellers has fallen away in recent years. The ongoing, flat-lining economy (since 2009) has not helped commercial enterprises justify spending budget on excessive travel experiences for small numbers of elite employees when other parts of the organization are being downsized. Even though it can be shown from an ROI perspective that travel is by far the most effective incentive reward, it has become socially and commercially unacceptable to spend lavishly on small numbers of employees. In many cases, although the enterprise has the cash reserves, it cannot be seen by others to be spending revenue earned in this way anymore. This does not appear to be the case in the United States where the most recent (2012) group travel statistics from Site (Society of Incentive Executives) seem to show that group reward travel is actually increasing by 10 per cent, year on year. However 'concentives' – a mix of conference, convention and incentive – seem to be on the rise in Europe to compensate for this decrease in overt spending, where the reward is combined with skills development. In this way such programmes are perceived as being a little more acceptable to other employees and stakeholders as a way to reward exceptional performance.

Customer satisfaction measures

When analyzing engagement going forward you need to create a sub-section of any survey for employed salespeople and ask slightly different questions of them than for office-based employees. It would be fine to ask questions about interaction with other employees but the questions would need to be in the context of salespeople being an internal customer rather than simply sitting alongside technical colleagues.

Monitoring customer perceptions of engagement values needs to differentiate between office-based administration staff and field staff because the degrees of daily interaction will be very different. It goes without saying that they should be measured against their own customer interface values, such as face-to-face meetings and presentations, rather than by e-mail or telephone, which is the likeliest first touch point for most administration employees. It would be inaccurate to publish 'trust' levels of office-based staff and field-based employees as if they were the same people doing the same job. Discovering that perceptions of trust were different or even diverging between customers and administration and customers and the employed sales team would be a pointer to remedial action to protect the integrity and authenticity of the engagement brand.

Channel engagement programmes

As soon as you step beyond the boundaries of the relatively closed, predictable world of employees you enter the arena of ambassadorship and advocacy. They are grand-sounding words, but they reflect the truth that such programmes rely on goodwill, give and take and trust rather than coercion, as the audience groups are not your employees. They cannot be forced to do what your organization wants. They cannot be 'let go' as the ultimate sanction for non-compliance.

What is ambassadorship? Here is an example from the London Underground public sector enterprise known as TfL (Transport for London), which runs 'the tube'.

CASE STUDY   TfL announcement to teachers about ambassadorship

Are you a teacher looking for ways to engage with your students? Would your students like to learn more about careers in engineering and transport planning? If so, you may be interested in our Ambassadorship Programme. Engineers and planners are one of the backbones of TfL but we face potential shortages of people with these specialist skills, particularly in Highways, Rail and Transport Planning.

To address this, we have partnered with the London Engineering Project (LEP) to find Ambassadors to give presentations and lead interactive activities within school classrooms. Our Ambassador Programme hopes to generate interest and

awareness of the engineering and planning professions among key stage 3 school students (11–13 years old) by using real engineers and planners as role models to influence the students' choice of subjects.

We ultimately hope to see more students coming into these professions in the future.

In this example TfL has a future need for engineers and logistics planners and wants to influence schoolchildren to consider a career in engineering, preferably with TfL, as far out as, say 10 years. It already knows that there is a current shortage of engineers in the UK.

Hoping for the best is not an effective recruitment strategy. TfL also knows that teachers can exercise a strong influence over the future career choices of their pupils. On their part teachers are often looking for ways to add value to their lesson content to develop their pupils in practical ways and to provide variety. The ambassadors are not paid but there is satisfaction in being able to deliver new material that others may not be aware of. The ambassador concept also taps into the altruistic nature of vocational professions and causes where profit is not the main objective.

Advocacy for causes

Advocacy is similar although it is mostly associated with issues or causes that are of general benefit rather than for just one organization. Typically, raising money for charitable causes is advocacy. Enterprises may have touch points with advocacy through their CSR activities, where volunteers from within the organization and from the advocacy group work together to promote a wider benefit such as a cure for cancer. If you are a vendor that uses natural resources such as wood as part of your manufacturing process it would make sense to have links with an advocacy group that protects the environment and helps to replace any natural resources used in the production process. In this way the enterprise can be seen to be aligning its brand values with something positive and 'giving back' rather than simply exploiting the natural environment.

The point about ambassadorship and advocacy is that they can be very powerful elements in strategic brand engagement because the positive brand engagement values of the organization can be transported into the wider community through altruistic activities and out-of-workplace projects. There is a commercial rationale too – to attract more customers at relatively little cost – but it is done in such a way that volunteers feel they are deriving a personal benefit as well, even if that is simply raising funds for a worthy cause. There has to be a fit with the sponsor's values, not just linking on a random basis with an advocacy brand. The purpose is to create a stronger message through the two organizations working together as partners, rather than one brand trying to outshine the other.

The ambassador/advocacy technique echoes many aspects of social media marketing in that the role of the organization is to be helpful and a 'good citizen', not just trying to sell something. Generation Y is very aware of product-pushing so such joint projects need to be carefully crafted so as not to attract the criticism of commercializing a cause. There has to be benefit for the partner organization otherwise you would simply be debasing your brand and eventually reducing your reach into your customer community. Reputation is easily damaged and hard to restore, so tread carefully.

Ambassadorship within enterprises

Offering both cash and non-cash incentives to non-employed channel salespeople and distributors is a common way to 'buy' share of the market, even if only for a brief period. This is particularly true when the distributor sells a number of similar and even competing products to retail outlets or other distributors. A standard programme is known as a 'spiff' or 'spif'. Its origins are somewhat obscure and many have tried to make the letters an acronym (sales promotion incentive fund?) It is a colloquial term for a bonus payment as a reward for selling a specific product, particularly in the electronics sector. The rewards could be cash or non-cash such as retail gift cards or credits. 'Spiff days' are when the sponsoring vendor visits a distributor's sales floor and offers instant, usually low value, rewards for vendor sales on that day or over a recent period. Salespeople promote the vendor's products to all their relevant customers on that day and receive rewards for doing so.

Longer-term spiffs

There are more sophisticated spiff variations such as hosted group travel programmes in which salespeople compete amongst each other over a longer period, say three or six months, and can qualify for a hosted group holiday package as a reward for sales for that specific vendor. There may be lower level rewards too, for those who do not qualify for the main travel incentive. It may be that the salespeople have to compete with other distributors on a national basis to qualify for the eventual travel reward. Although such spiff programmes have been around for a long time, vendors have always worried about the often disproportionate cost of 'buying' product loyalty in this way as invariably the benefits are very short-term and once the spiff period is over, sales drop off dramatically in favour of another vendor's products.

If salespeople find it easier to sell one vendor's products over another for technical or price reasons, then those products are more likely to be offered in the future. But it is not always a 'What's in it for me?' strategy. Most good salespeople will take the line of least resistance and would rather sell a 'branded' product they know all about than one with no market presence and no obvious technical features that would be of current interest to potential buyers.

Vendor loyalty and ambassador programmes

One way around this almost inevitable switching of loyalty to your nearest competitor when you have left the building is to instal an ambassador programme for independent channel employees. The essence of such programmes is that they are long term, often annual, and provide more than just incentives for short-term sales. Loyalty programmes often offer a stepped series of vendor benefits in return for more turnover. The benefits would include preferential buying rates, supply of merchandising material, privileged supply of new stock models and, most important, training of distributor/retail staff in new products' key features. This a good deal for both the distributor and the vendor but in the final analysis it is a commercial equation between getting the best buying-in price and any desirable extras to assist with the sell-in process. Distributors have to decide if it is worth taking a lower purchase cost to get the higher non-tangible benefits or a higher cost and scale down on the training/merchandising elements.

Ambassadorship is something different. In essence the distributors promote your products on your behalf for non-tangible benefits. There is, of course, a set-up and management cost for doing this, but the credibility of a third party promoting your products while still giving best advice or endorsement is a strategic brand activity that is hard to replicate with cash alone.

CASE STUDY   A typical ambassador programme

Here's how it works, using the example of a global mobile/cell phone vendor wanting to get more visibility within network provider stores. It already had volume sales agreements and runs non-cash incentives over specific periods during the year but it had not been able to get a significant share of the retail market using these traditional commercial routes. Chris Taylor of brand engagement consultancy FMI Group explains:

> *The vendor was keen to try new ways to get traction in this highly competitive market so we suggested they try an ambassador programme. The retail salespeople are all early adopters of new mobile technology and like nothing better than to show off new features to their colleagues and customers. We know that when retail customers are not sure which handset to purchase they tend to ask the sales assistant what handset they use themselves. If this could be the vendor's latest product, then there is a good chance that higher sales will develop.*

But simply handing out expensive, new products is a costly exercise and depending on the integrity of the salespeople the vendor had found in the past that these cutting-edge products soon found their way on to eBay or similar auction sites and the sales assistants simply kept the cash. This did not achieve the purpose of the products acting as demonstrators and damaged the vendor brand as new and often unreleased products were finding their way into the hands of consumers through unauthorized channels at knock-down prices.

We had to think of ways to protect the brand but also to get the product adopted by enthusiastic sales assistants to be used at the point of sale. One way to do this was to 'invite' retail store managers to nominate one or two vendor ambassadors per store who would receive, free of charge, a high-specification new handset, technical training and invitations to seminars to help them present the features of the vendor's product in an effective way, both to consumers and their retail colleagues. In addition they would receive recognition for their efforts. In return the ambassadors would be expected to use the vendor app on the handset to feed back market information, respond to colleague queries via the social networking channel and use the app to download technical product information to pass on to their consumers and colleagues.

The vendor was able to prevent resale of the handsets on auction sites by restricting its use to the known ambassadors through passwords and other security protocols. The market information was displayed in the vendor's central marketing department on a large TV screen so that all the brand managers could see what the market was saying in real time, rather than having to wait for local field managers to send in their regular update reports.

An unusual side-benefit of having handsets and tablets available in-store, with closed loop access, was the ability to train other retail colleagues informally on the vendor's products when there was downtime, thereby saving significant amounts on taking time out of the store to attend training seminars in local hotels, which was the old way of doing things. The vendor was also able to supply consumer-applicable video of key features to be viewed via the device rather than having to rely on in-store merchandising units or the receipt of updated centrally-resourced marketing materials.

The app was supported by a web microsite which integrated app activity with a points-mean-prizes reward site, to encourage regular interaction and activity when retail salespeople had desktop access.

Ambassador results

During the first 12 months of the vendor's ambassador programme the over-arching website had an average visit time of over six minutes, with ambassador visitors viewing eight pages per visit. Almost 800 ambassadors were recruited nationally with 40 per cent engaging in 'splash' activity (regular comments on commercial or technical issues) on a weekly basis. The following year 18 per cent more ambassadors were successfully recruited with a corresponding increase in online and wireless activity. It is almost impossible to measure ROI for this element of the activity as microsite visits do not translate directly into handset sales increases. But as a supporting activity in a competitive market the vendor feels it has the edge in retail 'share of mind' which far outweighs, dollar for dollar, any commercial improvement on product purchase rates or visits they may make to the stores in any given marketing cycle.

Applications for other sectors

Ambassadorship works best when the channel's employees or consumers are genuinely enthusiastic about the products they are demonstrating for free. This is an easy concept to apply to consumer electronics where they are selling desirable products that most people would like to own, but there are other sectors where similar concepts of unpaid/recognition-only advocacy exist, even if there is a commercial benefit for the sponsor but none for the ambassadors.

Arts ambassadorship is a good example. 'Friends' of your local theatre or art gallery is an effective way to encourage additional paid-for visitors at relatively little cost. People with like-minded interests tend to cluster together at similar events, so enrolling people as 'friends' enables the sponsor to reach potential new visitors. The biggest single cost in most membership-based organizations is that of acquiring new members, so if it can be done at minimal cost it becomes a very effective way to market the brand.

CASE STUDY   Glasgow 2014 Commonwealth Games

A G Barr, manufacturers and distributors of the Scottish soft drink Irn-Bru, included an engagement programme for volunteers as part of its planning for its sponsorship of the athletes' drinks throughout the Games. The CEO Roger White commented: 'Glasgow 2014 is massively exciting, whether you are taking part, volunteering or watching. The Games will bring something extraordinary to a very special city and we are delighted to be playing our part in that.'

Part of A G Barr's engagement programme with the local community is to leverage the goodwill of volunteers to help out with logistical tasks in the smooth running of the Games but also to project a clear brand image of A G Barr as a respected member of the local community, which will help with sales as well as recruitment in the aftermath of the Games. This is a classic example of advocacy at work with clear benefits for the sponsor at all levels.

Advocacy tends to be more altruistic than ambassadorship and is normally connected with raising discretional charity or benevolent funds. But from a strategic brand engagement viewpoint the activity needs to support the sponsor's brand, not jar with it. It makes sense for a life insurance organization to promote advocacy for a medical or wellbeing charity as this would complement the 'care' brand value that insurance enterprises espouse. An oil enterprise could legitimately defend promoting advocacy for eco projects on the basis that it needs to 'restore' the environment to its natural state after extraction has taken place. But it would be very odd for an automotive vendor to support advocacy of public transport if the main aim of public transport was to do away with personal transport. There has to be consistency in ambassadorship and advocacy otherwise the brand becomes damaged and lack of authenticity is perceived.

Avoiding bribery and sharp practice for ambassadors

In recent years there has been some progress in aligning commercial practices with global standards on bribery and corruption. Although payments in kind for advocacy by organizations appear to be relatively innocent, all stakeholders need to tread a careful and informed line between what is acceptable and what is not.

The Foreign Corrupt Practices Act (FCPA) became law in the United States as far back as 1977, outlawing the receipt of bribes by any US organization for contractual favours when implementing public sector projects. After many years working with the OECD (Organization for Economic and Social Development) Convention on Bribery and lobbying for change, the principles behind the FCPA have now been adopted by most Western governments to create a level playing field for international tenders. In the UK the Bribery Act 2010 made it a criminal offence for the first time, rather than a corporate offence, for any individuals to engage in bribery, with possible custodial sanctions for individuals who organize the payment, in cash or kind, not just the person who sanctions it.

In the ambassador example above the mobile handsets were lent to the independent employees rather than given away, so as not to contravene the new bribery laws. This principle would also apply to any 'informal' payments, such as gift cards, that ambassadors may receive as a result of their advocacy. Any benefits in kind for advocates need to be openly discussed and be published as part of the engagement initiative so as to be compliant with any national and international corruption legislation.

Brand match vs brand clash

When engaging non-employed salespeople your own internal brand consistency is more important than adapting your brand to the channel organization. Two separately owned enterprises can never be totally compatible from a brand perspective – otherwise the brand would not be commercially unique and therefore authentic – but they do need to be as aligned as possible. According to the Conyngham Performance Group, strategic brand engagement with the channel happens best when the following criteria are met.

Reduction in channel conflict

This means the vendor setting a clear policy about who you give preferential deals and rates to, what level of promotional support you are prepared to give, not asking a partner to provide service when there has been no sale and respecting geographical boundaries between channel partners. In brand engagement terms it means asking the partner to accept an ambassador programme and monitoring how supportive they will be in the field of what you, as the vendor, are attempting to do.

Making it easy for them to sell for you

The vendor needs to provide technical training and systems support so that the channel partner can integrate easily with the vendor to make sales. If your brand prides itself on 'simplicity', how simple is it for your channel partners to administer orders from you and get product out to their channel customers?

Making it easy for consumers to buy from them

With the number of ways to buy increasing all the time, the vendor needs to think if the channel partner has the best possible online and offline routes for the vendor's specific products. If the brand engagement strategy says the vendor will be available 24/7 for customer queries, this should also apply to the channel.

Working on a channel partner brand fit

You may have to educate new partners in your values, especially if they have been revised and the 'old values' no longer apply. This is particularly true of heritage brands that may have been sold off to new owners who have different views about service and product reliability. This means workshops, new downloadable technical materials, online statements from senior people, senior management briefings and conferences. If one of your brand engagement aims is to align brand values across your organization, it should also apply to keeping the channel up to date with brand thinking so as not to cause a mismatch between expectations and actual commercial behaviour.

Customer advocacy

Some consumer products inspire fanatical advocacy. Automotive manufacturers have known this for many years and use the phenomenon to obtain repeat purchases. In recent times electronic devices of all kinds have their followers, sometimes giving loyalty where repeat purchases are not always deserved. Apple has been very skilful at nurturing a loyal customer base who will not only buy whatever product Apple produces next but will recommend such products to everyone they come across. This is the ultimate goal of all brand managers: getting existing customers to recommend your products to their friends and acquaintances for no payment. It certainly makes your media costs tumble and reduces the need to spend budget on paid-for media if the public will do this job for you at no cost.

Within a business-to-business context business customer advocacy is also the main goal of brand engagement programmes. If the organization has an admirable brand and its employees are engaged with the values to the level of, say, 80 per cent then it makes sense to try and replicate that performance with non-employees – if the values are authentic and make sense, business partners could benefit from the same efficiencies and product satisfaction that comes from the product delivering what it says it will deliver, wherever you happen to come across it in the supply chain.

By extension they will then tell others in the supply chain that the best vendor/product is X. When they move jobs they will take this brand experience with them and continue to recommend this product, even if they no longer have a business use for it. They will remember trusting what the vendor did, how it always delivered on its promises and how reliable the product was. Unwittingly they become unpaid ambassadors for the product and the organization that produced it, even though they no longer have any direct commercial contact with the enterprise.

Closing the brand engagement circle

So, having undertaken a thorough examination of the organization's values, trained your employees in the new brand values, taken that package of engagement activities to the distribution channel through an ambassador programme and explored all the possible avenues for advocacy through CSR links, it's time to see if the consumer can be engaged with your brand in a more meaningful way than simply through a cash or credit card transaction.

Engaging through experiences

09

> *The growth of experiential has been at a time of ever increasing marketing 'noise' and competition for the consumer's attention. We are all now subjected to literally thousands of marketing messages every day. As mobile and web communication have been added to the marketing mix this level of noise is only getting louder.*
>
> **(INSTITUTE OF PROMOTIONAL MARKETING, UK)**

The internet has made us all more connected, whether we like it or not. Due to the fragmentation of media, particularly social media, consumers can now engage with brands in a much more direct and individual way. From e-mails, texting and online surveys to 'installations', consumers are now being involved with brand experiences more frequently than ever before. The old reliance on mass media marketing in the developed economies is reducing as audiences turn away from their TVs and spend more of their leisure time with a wide array of other electronic devices. Many of these techniques are only just being formalized (you will discover this in the next chapter, on engagement and social networking) as ways to engage with their tech-savvy audiences.

From a strategic brand engagement viewpoint such techniques can apply equally to employees and the channel. Employees are consumers too so it is not surprising that they expect consumer-standard marketing, even if it comes from their employer. The 'dead hand' of internal marketing done on the cheap is fortunately on the way out. Digital creation and distribution of materials is almost cost-free in many circumstances so there is no longer an excuse to produce substandard marketing materials just because it is an internal message.

To reach employees on an individual basis and actively ask for their personal involvement in the brand is something new and surprisingly effective. Employees are not obliged to give you their discretional time outside working hours and often will ignore internal messages, if they are 'too busy', but when they do, you should make the most of it as an engagement specialist. In this chapter we will explore a new marketing phenomenon known as 'experiential' and how this could be used to improve employee, channel and ambassador engagement. E-mails and Monday morning briefings are all very well, but there is lots more you could be doing to engage with your main audiences of employees and distributors.

What is 'experiential'?

'Experiential' in this context is an event, online or offline, that trials a product, message or attitude outside the confines of mass media.

You could say that mobile product trialling has always been with us. The manufacturers of the Winchester Rifle ran 'frontier road shows' in the 1800s, taking their product to where it was needed most at the time. The Great Exhibition of 1851 – The Great Exhibition of the Works of Industry of all Nations – held at Crystal Palace, London, was attended by 6 million visitors and made enough surplus to fund the building of the Victoria and Albert Museum, The Science Museum and the Natural History Museum, which are major tourist attractions to this day. It was the first in a series of World Fairs that were the precursors of the modern global exhibitions industry.

During the 20th century various developments in promotional engagement to showcase and demonstrate new products formed the nucleus of what is now termed 'field marketing'. The Field Marketing Council (FMC) of the Direct Marketing Association (DMA) in the UK defines field marketing as 'measurable, face-to-face brand development and customer relationship management through using highly trained people'. Similar trade bodies exist throughout the developed world, representing marketing organizations that advise on taking the brand physically to where the customers are, rather than using mass media and hoping consumers will visit retail outlets at some stage in the future.

The Experiential Marketing Forum

The Experiential Marketing Forum, based in the United States, is a practitioner, member-based organization that specializes in consumer engagement through live events and activities. Its definition is very similar to that of the FMC, with the addition of a specific sales focus:

> The term 'experiential marketing' refers to actual customer experiences with the brand/product/service that drive sales and increase brand image and awareness. It's the difference between telling people about features of a product or service and letting them experience the benefits for themselves.

The organization runs an impressive series of online and offline development sessions to improve knowledge of the main disciplines and it comes as no surprise that many involve social media planning and evaluation techniques.

Typically, experiential marketing includes promotional activity by merchandisers and promoters that mainly happens face-to-face with prospective consumers (or distributors) to support or even replace traditional mass media advertising. There are a number of activities field marketers are involved with:

- *Promoters*: providing outsourced sales personnel to either visit businesses to sell and gain distribution of products and services, or to sell direct to the end user – typically conducted face-to-face in consumers' homes, distributors' offices or in retail premises and shopping malls.

- *Merchandising*: placing point of sale (POS) materials, typically in retail stores, to coincide with specific campaign timings. This could consist of wall posters, pull-ups, hanging banners, miniature flags and other in-theme decorations to indicate where the 'experience' is taking place.

- *Auditing*: measuring and reporting on the status of a client's products in retail outlets (in terms of their availability, promotion, price, POS placement, etc). This measurement aspect is often undertaken by research specialists who can measure whatever part of the experiential process you think is important. A link is then made from the metrics of the event to the change in knowledge, attitude or sales behaviour at some future date.

● *Mystery calling and mystery shopping*: measuring and reporting covertly on customer service and sales standards at the 'moment of purchase'. This technique is mostly used in retail environments where consumers can be anonymous, but is of less use in the channel where most buyers and suppliers are known.

● *Sampling and demonstrating*: providing consumers with a simple sample or demonstration of a product. What you can and cannot do is dictated by local legislation and is largely shaped by cultural attitudes to marketing practices. Each European country has its own codes of conduct, so what is acceptable in the UK, for example, is not necessarily legal in France or Germany.

● *Road shows and events*: where a promotional activity is created that can be replicated at different venues, to more fully engage the audience with the overall brand, not necessarily to trial or sell a product or service. In some circumstances training and distributor development is handled through road shows and so such a technique becomes a key way for the manufacturer to engage with its various channels on an individual basis, rather than through more remote media.

Not all of these activities could be deemed to be 'experiential' as some have their roots in the market research industry. But we could say that experiential marketing includes specific brand events where the audience experiences the brand directly through its products or indirectly through association, such as an entertainment or commercial sponsorship.

Attempts at formal definitions of a technique that is so new will all fail and be out of date in a matter of months but the Experiential Committee of the IPM (UK) has come up with a working summary for now (2013): 'A live and interactive marketing discipline, which builds positive emotional sensory engagement between a brand and its consumer.' In other words, experiential marketing is the interaction between a brand and a consumer (which could equally be an employee or distributor) representing the brand and product's key emotional and functional benefits and stimulating the senses to achieve a deeper and longer-lasting impact. The key benefit is that it gives brands the chance to prove or demonstrate the promises they make in other media. But what typically is an experiential event?

The blossoming experts in this field are very creative in the types of event they run; here is a list of typical 'experiences':

- *Branded events.* Mass consumer events taking place in indoor or outdoor locations that become a 'property' of the brand. Examples include O2 Wireless Festival, Innocent Fruitstock and the Budweiser Super Bowl.

- *Branded installations.* Branded 'stands' in indoor or outdoor public spaces manned by promotional staff that attract consumers to interact with a brand. Examples include Nivea Outdoor Office in city parks and the Vodafone stand at London Heathrow.

- *Creative sampling.* Free product distribution executed in a creative manner. Examples include Twiglets, the pre-packaged snack, handing out free packs by promoters in giant Twiglet costumes and Red Bull beverage teams driving branded Volkswagen Beetle cars.

- *Live stunts.* One-off live stunts designed to attract mass consumer and media attention. Examples; Trafalgar Square, London being filled with over 100 grave headstones for Amnesty International, flash mob gatherings created through social media which support brand messages, and 'charity challenges' run before and during intervals at national sports events.

- *Live performance.* Teams of actors delivering a live performance to communicate a brand message. Example; barbershop singers located in supermarkets to support the launch of a new bread.

- *Pop-up retail.* Miniature portable installations, mobile vehicles or fixed spaces used by brands to create temporary promotional stores or gathering places. Examples; Nike customized mobile vans demonstrating and selling training shoes at major track races and the Sony Mobile Xperia bus that toured major UK locations in 2013 offering ambassadors privileged training on the new Xperia mobile phone.

Employee and channel experiential events

What kind of events would be appropriate for employee or channel engagement? It is not uncommon for new products or services to be showcased in vendor reception areas so that employees and regular visitors can see what is new and have the brand image or some new initiative reinforced. Some vendors run annual or even quarterly product showcases, often on site, in marquees or other temporary structures so that not only is there more room to demonstrate larger products but private areas where distributors can discuss details of any collaboration that may result from the showcase event. Human resources often favour the employee canteen or private dining areas to exhibit new products and employee campaigns such as links with charities. In such a relaxed, 'selling-free' zone it is more likely that most employees will be exposed to the new messages that can then be followed up online via desktop systems or via cell phone messages.

Digital amplification

The ability to extend the reach (size of the audience exposed to the activity) of experiential activity into digital spaces – websites, microsites and social media channels like Facebook, Digg, Flickr, LinkedIn and Twitter – has seen a revolution in the experiential world. Continuing engagement from the live environment into the digital world has given experiential greater longevity as a channel and, most important of all, increased the perceived reach of campaigns. The attraction is that specific audiences can be reached for specific employee and distributor activities, although you need to bear in mind that sometimes the information is 'open channel' and you need to be happy that others, including your competitors, may see it.

Experiential marketing has been criticized as being an expensive channel by way of the cost per interaction with the consumer when compared with traditional broadcast media. This is old-school marketing thinking. The quality and type of interaction facilitated through experiential is vastly different to a broadcast channel like TV advertising. Experiential marketing creates engaging content for digital platforms to use to start conversations with consumers and professional advocates such as bloggers and ambassadors. A strong, mutually beneficial marketing relationship exists between the multiple channels to market.

Effective experiential campaigns should always include an amplification strategy. The only way to ensure maximum ROI is to include amplification ideas and to measure their effectiveness. Table 9.1 shows the most common amplification methods and a brief idea of how you could approach measurement. It is not an exhaustive list and there are many methods of measuring each. For the purposes of designing a thorough evaluation model you must understand what tactics are available to achieve amplification and which ones deliver on your objectives and campaign KPIs.

TABLE 9.1 Experiential amplification and relevant measurement techniques

Amplification method	Measurement technique
Online media	Online reach
	Impressions
	Click-through rates
Digital/social media	Web traffic
	Number of comments
	Social media followers
	Sentiment analysis
	Word of mouth
Sales promotion	Competition entries
PR, internal	PR reach, impressions
	Share of online conversation

SOURCE: Unpublished study notes for the experiential diploma module, Institute of Promotional Marketing, UK

For instance, you may use internal print and online media to raise awareness of a campaign (and therefore the brand) internally and drive traffic to a specific event or activation. You might then choose to 'broadcast' to amplify your event message at the time of activation (increasing your brand or issue recall amongst your target audience, whether internal or external). Finally, it might be a good idea to follow up the live conversation by driving a social media call to action, ensuring that you engage word of mouth (WOM) and re-contact active participants with the main messages, or ask for ambassador support.

From unaware to loyal

Experiential events can be clearly targeted to specific groups in specific places, such as shopping malls and town centre spaces. Audiences are encouraged to attend an experiential event through timely and relevant social media messages via mobile phones or tablets. The main objective of the experiential marketer is to take participants from being unaware of your brand or message to loyal, in stages. This could include awareness, familiarity, active consideration and eventually purchase/attitude change. Loyalty would equate to habitual/repeat purchase or a discernible shift in attitude. Purchase is clearly the main goal for marketing campaigns, which could be online or offline, so the benefits for experiential are cross-platform future sales or attitude change, not just those confirmed sales or opinions changed at the event itself.

Measuring experiential activities

So, we are planning to engage with employees and/or the channel with 'live' promotional events to supplement the push advertising or brand promotion we may be producing. They may be one-off projects, but they are more likely to be repeated at various locations to enable you to reach as many employees and distributors as possible. But how do you assess whether the benefits outweigh the cost, when compared with more traditional ways to engage with your employee or channel universe?

In Spring 2009, Jack Morton Worldwide (**www.jackmorton.com**), the communications agency, questioned the ROI from experiential marketing activities. In the survey of UK senior marketers, 76 per cent said that the lack of any robust measurement of ROI for experiential marketing was a significant barrier to their use of such campaigns. Measuring the success of an experiential campaign – and ultimately the ROI for the brand that is being promoted – is certainly more challenging than for most established marketing activities. This is because, by their nature, experiential campaigns tend to be long term rather than short term in their effect. No marketer would ever advertise in any given medium, look at sales the next day, and declare it a success or a failure. The events need to happen over a defined period with a specific audience and then movements in attitudes or sales tracked over the following weeks or months.

Specific metrics of measurement

Let's assume you have decided to run a series of experiential events for employees to help them engage with the brand more fully than could be achieved through more traditional methods. The measures you could use to build a case for effectiveness are as follows.

Event attendance

How many employees attended the various sessions and what percentage of total employees on the site was this? Did it vary by time of day or day of week? How long did they stay at the event on average? Did they come in team groups or as individuals? Did they recommend other employees to come along as a result of their initial attendance?

Opportunity to engage

Depending on the activity (often people come to watch what others are doing rather than involve themselves) what level of active engagement was there? How many achieved the task or won the competition, expressed a desire to come again, etc? This could be measured by completing an online feedback form either at the event or later from their desktops or via a phone app. Some measurement experts say you should record both active engagement (such as trying the product or participating in a game) and passive engagement – those who stand by and watch. But analysis over many consumer events has shown that both types of attendee show equal propensity to tell others or engage in social media about the brand at some later stage. So being active or passive makes little difference to an event's success.

Demographics

What level of employee attended, were they supported by their line manager or team leader, were they old-stagers or relatively new recruits? Did the range of employees reflect the entire range of your workforce or were there significant departments missing, such as finance or engineering?

In isolation these numbers tell you little about the effectiveness of the events. But when compared across multiple sites or through online feedback and social media traffic at a later stage you can begin to measure which parts of the organization respond to this particular marketing approach and which do not. It is likely that incoming calls administration employees will always be positive about getting actively engaged in an 'event' happening in the office, but senior staff may need to be treated in a different way. The point is that experiential provides an opportunity for you to engage with your employee or channel audience in a completely new way, supported by digital media that perhaps did not exist in this format for corporates ten years ago.

Social media point the way

The old model of employee brand engagement through annual meetings, suggestion schemes and wall posters in the lunch room is broken. This is not to say they have done poorly over the years: some set-piece employee meetings have been superb examples of corporate theatre, creating great bonding exercises around key themes. Equally, pan-organization campaigns to 'cut costs' or 'improve service' have their place in the record books of sound communications programmes. Many have succeeded beyond expectations and certainly provided more benefit than they cost. But the introduction of social media and employee access to instant messaging has shaken up the human resources/marketing box to such an extent that just putting the Employee Handbook online is no longer good enough.

Experiential is yet another in a long line of marketing techniques that brand engagement specialists could adapt when thinking how to get the new message across to an increasingly brand aware and sceptical employee audience. Interaction is the watchword – opportunities to involve employees directly in 'events', supported by instant, online promotion, will be the way to reach full engagement in the future. But such events will have to be created and managed professionally with a backdrop of offline promotion, online media and slick activity logistics that support rather than diminish the brand. It will no longer be acceptable to say 'It's only for employees, so that will do.'

The improvement in communication devices and the rise in the use of social media provide a new challenge for anyone attempting to implement an engagement programme for large numbers of people. The next chapter looks at social networking in particular and why engagement professionals need to be aware of how the growing number of the workforce and consumers in general use social media to engage with each other and your brand throughout the day. This provides a new opportunity for leaders and managers to engage personally with every employee and advocate, but it also brings challenges to the normal way of doing things.

Engagement and social networking

10

Today's generation aren't interested in settling down to do just one task. When they work they're always open to communications from whomever might be interested in giving them a project... or a valuable piece of insight.

(SHULI GOLOVINSKI, 2011)

Generation Y is what marketers call those born between 1981 and 2000. They behave somewhat differently in the workplace to those who came before the internet was invented. Although we have dealt with communicating the employer brand internally (Chapter 7) the phenomenon of social networking and its part in engaging with the employees of the future need to be understood.

If you have no social media strategy for your employees or your channel partners you will have less and less engagement in future because this is how your new generation of managers currently operates and will continue to operate going forward. At the moment social media operate mostly in the non-professional sphere. But in time they will apply to the professional world as more B2B buyers become aware of reputations being built and possibly destroyed online within days, as happens in the public domain. If this does not interest you as a senior manager or VP, you can ignore this chapter, but you do so at your peril. Social media is the way employees will communicate with each other and their team leaders in the future. If you want to improve general levels of organizational engagement, senior managers need to understand how social media work and how to harness them for strategic brand engagement within a professional environment.

How did we get here?

Marketers talk a lot about Baby Boomers, Generation X and Generation Y (see Figure 10.1). This is shorthand for being responsive to generational attitudes to consumer issues, brands and, increasingly, technologies. Although the categories are age-related the general theory is that most (but by no means all) people of the same generation are affected in similar ways by changing technology and social attitudes.

FIGURE 10.1   Consumer generations

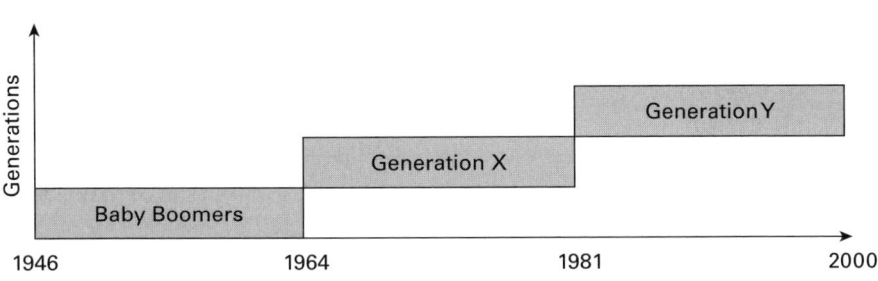

Baby Boomers were born after World War II in a time of rising prosperity. Consumer durables such as washing machines and TVs came within reach of average household budgets for the first time. The term 'teenager' was invented to account for newly-affluent young people who had disposable income and therefore were of great interest to marketers and those who sold products to younger people.

Generation X characterizes those who came after the Baby Boomers, an era that saw the rise of the internet, the dotcom bubble and entrepreneurship. Generation Y took advantage of all the technological developments of the 1970s and 1980s, particularly developments in mobile phone technology and internet connectivity. The generational differences of these three groups are important as they shape attitudes to technology usage, social media and feelings of inclusion or exclusion when it comes to mass communication. All large organizations will have representatives from all three generations in their workforce but their attitudes to communication and brand promotion will be different.

In the pre-internet era, HR and marketing activities, internal and external, were mostly conducted following C-suite level policy changes and subsequent analysis of large databases to send a communication to. Once you had identified your 'audience' the task was how best to communicate the idea, policy change or brand enhancement by pushing the message out to a static and waiting market. Once the communication was 'pushed' out, you would then survey those who received the message to check that they had perceived it in the way you imagined. If not, further push messages were then devised with more emphasis on correcting the misunderstandings.

The larger the audience, the more bland the message because being too detailed, too cute or too funny often results in misunderstandings. It was rare to ask for participation before the message was sent out. It was enough simply to show that the message had gone out and that, in the main, it was understood as intended.

Things moved relatively slowly due to the mechanical nature of the design, printing and publishing process. Instantaneous communication could only be effected by telephone and documents/data could only be exchanged by fax or sent by courier. Executives sent letters by mail and met face-to-face when important things needed to be discussed and agreed. Business travel was a key element of growth. International communication of information was problematic. Ambitions to become a 'cross-borders' organization required detailed planning and the deployment of nationals overseas, in much the same way that you might colonize a new country. It was a slow business... and business was slow.

The internet changed everything

All that changed with the commercial adoption of the internet and its handmaidens: e-mail and the worldwide web. The combination of an instant messaging service and the facility to transfer complex and data-rich documents at the same time has fuelled the pace at which things are now said, known and agreed. Initially organizations thought they could still maintain the old levels of confidentiality and security on which many commercial decisions are made – knowledge is power, after all – but YouTube, MySpace,

Twitter and Facebook changed the paradigm of how the new communication system was being used in practice. There was a world outside official work channels and information was being leaked about organizational activity, some true, some just hearsay or simply mischievous misinterpretation. That can be amusing but not if brands are damaged with falsehood and people lose their jobs.

A report by agency Universal McCann in 2008 showed that some 394 million people between the ages of 16 and 54 watched video clips online, 248 million people uploaded photographs and 184 million started their own blogs during that year. The numbers are immaterial in that they would be much higher now, pointing to a global phenomenon of ordinary consumers comfortable with new media software. We have all moved beyond the 'geek age' where everything seemed very complicated and hard to do and you needed experts to do it. Through intuitive software, technophobes of any age can now be connected.

Devices

During the same period how you connect with the worldwide web also changed. Business history is littered with positive-thinking individuals prone to making sweeping, but wrong statements about the future. Tom J Watson, former IBM CEO, who died in 1956, was famous for saying: 'I think there is a world market for about five computers.'

Today's 'computer devices' range from desktops, laptops and tablets to game consoles, wireless handsets, touch screens and more. There will be more mobile/cell phone subscriptions than people in the world by the end of 2014, according to a UN agency report. The International Telecoms Union predicts that subscriptions will pass 7 billion. There are currently 6.8 billion mobile subscriptions and 7.1 billion people. The 2013 ITU World Report found that more than a third of the global population is online. The Commonwealth of Independent States, the alliance of countries formerly in the Soviet Union, has the highest mobile penetration with 1.7 subscriptions for every citizen. With more mobile phones than people, you have to marvel at the human appetite for connectivity.

The crossover in the use of devices from social to commercial life happened in the mid-2000s when fixed desktop devices gave way to mobile laptops that enabled the user to employ the same device for both business and personal data exchange. With the advent of mobile handsets and tablets, for business or personal use, the switch was complete.

Most consumers now interchange their devices' access to the internet seamlessly, for business and personal use, throughout the day. Unless you have a draconian approach to internet access in the workplace most employees are online virtually all day for business and personal reasons, with personal or social sites sometimes stored on the desktop home page, just in case someone wants to get in touch in another way. There is no longer a clear communications distinction between being 'at work' and being available for non-work social contact with friends and relatives.

But the range of devices used is only half the story. True communication is facilitated by the ubiquitous presence of social media providing global access to your personal or professional circle, made even more complicated and ungovernable by the fact that colleagues and business contacts may also be 'friends'. Tension arises in employee and channel communications when one section of your audience is less adept at accessing a medium than others – people need to be sharing media platforms for branding to work effectively.

Social media

What is it?

But is social media nothing more than a technological replacement for letter-writing or phone calls? In one way it is, but with the twist that in the public domain just one communication can destroy an organization's reputation overnight. Reputation can no longer be left to 'the complaints department' and largely forgotten.

Brian Solis, a prolific US evangelizer on all things new media, coined a useful and detailed definition of social media which is worth analyzing:

> Social media is the democratization of information, transforming people from content readers into publishers. It is the shift from a broadcast mechanism, one-to-many, to a many-to-many model, rooted in conversations between authors, people and peers.

> (Solis, 2011)

Social media – Twitter, Facebook, LinkedIn – enable the participant/member to write to individuals or groups, attach pictures, link to other sites and to receive data, virtually instantaneously. Clearly some media have certain other functional or user characteristics: Twitter only carries text messages of up to 140 character spaces, for example. Flickr is designed to send pictures rather than words. LinkedIn is mostly about career descriptions of professional people you may come across in business. But they all allow individuals to 'publish' messages and information globally, virtually un-checked, as well as receive them. Individuals can now contact people on the other side of the world who they have never met but with whom they share a common business or organizational bond. The implications for communication and the marketing of brand messages to individuals and groups of like-minded people are enormous. It is no surprise that early adopters were journalists and celebrities who have a mutually beneficial reason to be in contact with large numbers of individuals on a daily basis, globally, to earn a living.

On the surface some social media comments may appear frivolous and inconsequential. Does anyone really care if some Hollywood star has just been to Walmart? The point is, if that star's daily activity is being followed by millions of people worldwide and he or she mentions your organization, then something trivial suddenly becomes a brand issue and a way to influ-ence consumer perceptions for very little marketing or communications spend. Social media comment can no longer be ignored, even if many tradi-tional organizations would like to do so. Pretending social media comment does not exist is no longer an option.

How should we communicate with social media?

While private individuals have been using social media models for some years, organizations have struggled to get to grips with the benefits, many being fearful of the potential for negative comments. As Brian Solis points out, 'monologue has given way to dialogue' and there is no way back. But the unrestricted right to broadcast a reply by consumers to millions of other consumers can cause organizations specific commercial problems. A com-plaint can no longer be contained within the 'customer service' department, pending a formal corporate reply some weeks later. Rebuttal, if required, needs to be quick, accurate, friendly and very possibly on the same day it was received.

CASE STUDY   JetBlue

In mid-February 2007 US low-cost carrier JetBlue had to cancel, reschedule then cancel again a number of flights due to exceptionally poor weather. Rather than deplane passengers it decided to leave them on board, pending an upturn in the weather conditions. In a previous era such decisions may have appeared in printed media the next day but it would have been a 'so-what?' story. But complaints gathered momentum across a number of social media sites within a few days and investors began to ask questions about JetBlue's business acumen.

The then CEO David Neeleman decided to confront the issue head-on and apologized publicly both in traditional print media and online. The company even posted a YouTube video to say sorry. What could have developed into a protracted stand-off between the organization and its potential customers was defused in a few days and consumers were impressed by JetBlue's 'authenticity' in admitting its errors. JetBlue now tweets flight delays and hosts a public group on Flickr on which customers are encouraged to send photos of themselves using JetBlue services, promoting dialogue with the organization rather than confrontation.

This mindset of dealing with brand issues online is a pointer to how the world is now interacting with brands through conversation. Following pressure on Twitter regarding a $50 carry-on charge for bicycles, JetBlue reversed this policy, again demonstrating that as an organization it is listening and is in dialogue with its consumers. It is hard to say how many extra customers it gained as a result of this policy reversal but it is unlikely that such a decision would have been made had social media activity not been available to bring such pressure to bear.

The principles of good social media handling are to recognize that the new marketing paradigm is dialogue not monologue and that marketing is now a 24/7 activity that requires constant attention and swift organizational responses. Social media are not going to go away so the organization needs to have a strategy to deal with them.

What social media sites should you use?

The social media industry is fond of promoting ever-more niche media in the hunt for 'the next big thing'. It's hard to get kudos for being in an exclusive club if everyone is a member. But commercially speaking, most organizations need to be part of the main social media visited by their current or potential consumers and their employee and channel partners. In the main, for now, this will be Facebook, Twitter, LinkedIn, Digg and Flickr. There will be different languages or national sites that have better consumer reach, but you need to start somewhere.

As with the main website-based internet, it is not enough just to create a social media site and sit back. Managing a social media presence requires you to 'optimize' your presence through links to various other social media sites through key words, video links and phrases. Social media is as much about listening as it is about posting so you need to know who is saying what about your organization. It may be that your advocates use a particular advocates' social site to discuss advocacy issues, in which case getting involved with the site or forum in a helpful way may be useful in keeping in touch with what advocates think of your brand and in encouraging more advocates to join you.

The strategic brand engagement element for employees and channel partners is to mirror the consumer activity on social media with internal activity, but adopting similar approaches to information exchange. So, a corporate Facebook site may well have links to all the usual organizational assets that a consumer can find but the stories and dialogue will be about issues closer to home, such as providing better customer service, employee canteen reviews or a progress update on new office building developments. For channel partners there could well be a channel partners' variation where outward facing service and delivery issues are developed and discussed in a non-marketing, helpful, episodic way – dialogue and stories, not monologue.

How do social media sites differ from the web?

We live in an era of the corporate website. For most consumer marketing this will do for now. It is the equivalent of the traditional printed product brochure, so social media brand presence needs to reflect the same values but in a more conversational, less buttoned-up way. It is a dialogue medium, designed to provoke conversation with consumers and employees/business partners. It is dynamic rather than fixed in time.

If your internal organization is mostly about 'direct customer service' the creative rationale for the site could be to show videos of some aspects of service from around the world and invite conversations from employees about some of the issues it raises. If you are a construction company a series of YouTube-style videos of 'good practice' from around the world with real employees talking about their issues on site and what they did about solving them would generate some interesting dialogue. There is no script. Let the medium do it for you. Inevitably, as in all conversations, there may be some bad experiences and you need to be able to deal with this.

An interesting alternative to Twitter for employees/the channel is Yammer. Participants on a Yammer account need to have a company e-mail and can converse with each other on a live basis but in a closed loop. Employees and business partners can be added and removed at will to cope with the usual 'leavers and joiners' of organizational life.

Pandora's box

In the same way that marketers would monitor consumer social media sites for negative comments, hoping to respond quickly and positively, it should be someone's job within internal marketing to monitor for negative employee or channel comments. Typically this person is known as a 'community manager' who may well be linked to the consumer site so that negative consumer comments can be relayed to the relevant internal departments. For employees the community manager is able to steer dialogue towards issues the organization would like to clarify, without doing formal research. In addition he or she would become involved with negative comments with a view to resolution or at least closure. Many organizations shy away from social media sites in the mistaken belief that it would open up a Pandora's box of negative issues they would rather not air publicly. The point is that if there is a real issue within social media sites, it will be discussed anyway, so you need to have a damage limitation plan rather than no plan at all.

There have been several cases on Twitter in recent years where successful cases for libel have been brought by organizations against employed or channel individuals who have been tempted to say things online they would not normally say in writing or in public using traditional media. It has to be remembered that just because 'friends' online tend to say what they think to each other socially at the moment, this is not acceptable in the public domain and never has been, where commercial reputations and livelihoods are at stake. It is likely that perceptions of social media being just 'personal' are likely to change as society moves towards more open sharing of private information. In the same way that most organizations now have an internet policy regarding proprietary information, it is common for this to be extended to social media when conducted in the public domain or on behalf of an organization.

Typical public-facing social media policies now include declaring who you are ('an employee of X organization'), not disclosing confidential organizational information, not asking for confidential data from a respondent, not putting them in direct touch with another consumer, not making up answers (check first), saying sorry if you got it wrong, adding value, not bad mouthing other suppliers. This is far removed from the informal interactive style of most personal social media sites but still something that many employees have yet to get to grips with when it comes to managing corporate reputations online.

Twenty-first century schizoid man

There is no doubt that Robert Fripp (of prog rock King Crimson fame) was not thinking about social media in 1969 when he penned the phrase '21st century schizoid man'. But it neatly describes a dilemma of today's workers. In July, 2008 Linda Stone wrote in *Business Week*: 'Continuous partial attention describes how many of us use our attention today... To pay continuous partial attention is to pay partial attention continuously. It is motivated by a desire to be a live node on a network... and to be connected.'

The proliferation of devices means that most people are now encouraged to adopt different persona, even within the same minute, depending on which device we are using or what community we are communicating with. It also promotes a tendency, socially, to flit from device to device and issue to issue, possibly not resolving any of them. But what about the professional communicators?

Should the community manager engage in social media in his or her own right or as a representative of the organization? Many commentators say that the key to a successful online presence is authenticity. This works if you are speaking to friends and acquaintances, but not on behalf of an organization although you can still be an 'authentic' employee. By definition, an employee is acting on behalf of the employer so the communication is sincere in that the job is one of influence and professional persuasion. There are many online consultancies that have various systems to steer online conversations to the benefit of the sponsoring organization without appearing to be pushing a specific product. So there is still an element of planning and manipulation even if the impression is one of being open and sincere. But what to do is mostly common sense and follows the performance improvement model:

- Research your online community... external or internal.
- Listen to what they are discussing.
- Identify the 'social beacons' (bloggers, ambassadors) who can help you with your cause.
- Gather any useful tips and tricks to improve your performance internally.
- Make altruistic and useful contributions, if you can.
- Prioritize action: not everything needs to be actioned right now.
- Route comments to the right internal departments.
- Reward contributors with inside (but cleared) information and recognize their contribution by publicly thanking them.

Bloggers

One way around the sincere/insincere problem is to employ professional bloggers to engage with your audiences. This may be a good solution for the channel and advocates who will always be somewhat sceptical of paid employees offering 'independent advice'. Webloggers number in their millions and range from the sublime to the ridiculous. Technorati.com is a good first place to look for who might be blogging about your particular industry and therefore a good place to find professional bloggers who may work on your behalf to mention your products to the community you want to influence.

Large organizations could appoint their community manager to be the official internal blogger for the organization. *The Director*, a UK monthly magazine for senior managers, reviewed current practice and featured Suzi Williams, brand director BT, the telephone utilities company, who writes the BT blog in an amusing and off-the-wall style, avoiding industry jargon

(Maxwell, 2013). The aim is to engage with the audience in a light-hearted but internally-informed way. By being sincere and writing 'from the heart' even the sponsored organizational blog can be read regularly.

Trust and authenticity are the keys to a credible blog. Most people can spot 'advertorial' when they read it so it is vital to create an element of honesty between the reader and the writer. If a blog is funded by and written by corporate employees you should make it clear in the notes or the introduction that this is so. Most readers will respond positively if you are upfront from the outset. If the blogger is a genuinely independent writer a corporate sponsor will have to accept that from time to time there may be some criticism – but this only makes praise even more effective. Being straightforward with the readers is the only way that social media can operate well. Senior executives need to be aware that, as in all marketing, blogging has its risks when communicating complicated ideas to the wider, non-professional world.

Professional help

The quickest way to establish a social media presence for your internal or external audience is to pay for it. Just like advertising or indeed any promotional activity intended to influence or persuade, there is a lot to learn. Social media is a new phenomenon and although there are some sensible, logical ways forward it is not yet a mature way to market. Some of the 'rules' may be a little blurred and are still being refined. In the final analysis a human being has to sit down and plan activity, then do it. This all takes time and time, as we know, is money. So getting professional help is one way to kick-start your own employee social media.

There is no doubt that the use of social media in business will increase as what started as an amateur, non-professional communications activity between individuals is now having a significant effect on how consumers view mainstream products and services. Analysis of blogging topics shows that 90 per cent of blogs are about music, books and brands. Reputations can be made and broken very quickly, depending on online comment. In terms of strategic brand engagement this is a communications channel that cannot be ignored because your employees are also communicating with each other in social media, perhaps saying what they really think about the organization, rather than in the formal team briefings and official reports more familiar to

Baby Boomers, many of whom are still in charge of the internal communications media. So the quicker strategic planners get on the right page with social media the better for both the organization and those who deliver the brand on its behalf.

Social media presents one of the biggest brand engagement challenges to managers today. Generation Y use social media to organize their lives away from the office and increasingly to connect with business colleagues on both business and social issues and the central importance of informal, always-on, instant communication means it will become the medium of choice going forward (until something new comes along). If you want to communicate your brand to all ages of employees and your channel partners you need to consider how to square the circle of social media-savvy employees and those less comfortable with it.

So, assuming the brand is being communicated through all the relevant channels to your audiences the next thing to consider is whether examples of exceptional engagement should be rewarded and recognized formally. Would there be any performance advantage in saying well done to those who become fully engaged?

Rewards, recognition and respect

11

"Applauding success and forgiving failure...

(CHARLES HANDY, 1999)

What gets rewarded, gets done, as the saying goes. At some point in the strategic brand engagement cycle there will be an opportunity to reinforce new behaviours with rewards and public recognition. Many organizations already have reward programmes for new suggestions and ideas; others recognize outstanding individual and team performance through 'best in month' schemes and other annualized systems. They often stand alone as internal comms or human resources programmes whose origins remain obscure. They seem to always have been there and are usually unloved and uncared for and rarely tied in to any overall commitment to specific values or corporate ethics. Often they are the first expense to be culled when cost-cutting is on the agenda and before you know where you are you have no 'channels' that could be used to communicate with employees and others about the values of the business. Few have constructed such programmes deliberately as part of a strategic brand engagement scheme, but this is exactly what they are; but once they are gone, they are gone and the engaged become ever more disengaged.

Recognition and reward activities can also apply to channel partners and advocates to complete the strategic brand engagement loop. There are differences in application, of course, but all such programmes attempt to identify above-average performance, publicly recognize that the achievement was unusual and, in many but not all instances, have a reward attached. The overriding purpose of reward and recognition programmes is to encourage the most engaged to engage even more (becoming internal ambassadors for the brand, possibly) and to communicate to those less engaged that there are positive personal outcomes if you are prepared to make some effort.

People only work harder for more money

It was Dr Johnson's opinion in the 18th century that 'No man but a block-head ever wrote, except for money.' It is a common fallacy that persists in business that people only make extra effort for more income. In fact motivation theory shows that when operating above survival or poverty levels – in other words almost all people who work regularly in the developed world – social status and peer group recognition are much more motivational than cash. It has also been shown that offering non-monetary rewards rather than cash is more effective for promoting and recognizing higher performance, even though their cash values may well be equal.

A good example of this is a study of performance related pay (PRP) by Jensen and Murphy, University of Southern California, 1990, cited by *US Business Week*, where the relationship between remuneration of 2,000 senior executives across 1,200 organizations and corporate performance was compared. The study concluded that there was no direct correlation between PRP and corporate stock market performance; moreover 'executives tend to be overpaid for bad performance and underpaid for good performance.'

Cash vs non-cash

Despite the academic evidence many organizations still persist with cash programmes because this is what participants tell them they want whenever reward choices are researched. But the opposite is true: participants actually make more effort for non-cash rewards.

CASE STUDIES   Mazda

Amongst several case studies that compare cash incentives to non-cash payments the Mazda Motor Inc example stands out. Mazda Motor was planning an incentive to motivate its dealers to sell out B-Series trucks. The dealers were divided about which kind of incentive would produce the best result from its 2,000 managers and 6,000 sales executives. Some were adamant that only a cash bonus per unit sale would shift the 'metal' from the forecourt. Others suggested non-cash rewards such as merchandise or holiday travel. A hosted trip to Aspen, Colorado was offered for the 15 top sales managers nationally. But the decision whether to offer sales people cash or something tangible for above-target sales was unresolved.

The King Solomon solution

Senior management at Mazda met and decided to test the theory that non-cash works better than cash by initiating a straight split. Half the sales people were enrolled in the incentive scheme where they could earn $75 for every unit sale above target. The other half were offered a choice of merchandise from a rewards catalogue, but with the same value of incentive per unit sale. In addition both groups could call a toll-free number after each sale was completed and claim rewards on a random basis to the value of between $10 and $250.

The results were astonishing and yet again showed that when basic needs are met, non-cash rewards outperform cash rewards by a substantial factor. The non-cash group consistently sold more than the cash-only group regardless of the size of the dealership. By the end of the campaign period the cash group had increased their sales by just 2.13 per cent. The non-cash group had increased their base performance by 15.65 per cent.

An emotional response to tangibles

Post-campaign research revealed that the low-volume dealers were not enthused by just $75 for every additional truck sold as they calculated that they would not be able to sell the extra volume to make it worthwhile after deductions. However, those in the non-cash group could clearly identify in personal and family terms what their rewards could be and worked towards that goal, almost regardless of the monetary value. Mazda's own post-campaign research concluded: 'A reasonable assumption is that the emotional impact of an offer of tangible rewards, such as merchandise or travel, is more powerful from a behavioural-change point of view than an offer of the equivalent sum of money.'

CASE STUDY   Student incentives

A further example comes from the academic world. Scott Jeffrey, assistant professor of management sciences based at the University of Waterloo, Ontario in 2004 published the results of an experiment undertaken at the University of Chicago. Student participants were invited to take part in a word game in pursuit of an incentive. One group had no incentive for success; another group was rewarded with cash; the third group could qualify for a therapeutic massage of varying length, depending on their performance. The market values of the rewards were equal. After the word game exercise the massage group was then asked if they would have preferred the cash to the massage and 78 per cent said they would. However, the relative performances showed that while the cash group performed 14.6 per cent better than the no-incentives group, the massage group performed 38.6 per cent better than the no-incentive group, so more than twice as big an improvement.

Following up with qualitative analysis of the reasons, the groups felt that it was difficult to justify spending the cash on a massage but would be perfectly happy to receive a massage as a reward. The study suggests that people work harder for tangible, aspirational rewards than for cash alone. Participants will often say that what they want is money but they perform better for tangibles, so simply doing what participants say they want is not always the wise thing to do.

Practical reasons for using non-cash rewards are that retail cards, travel and other tangibles can be bought at discounts whereas cash is cash, and recognition items are not contractual. This means that you can change them or even withdraw them without having to present the case to a works union or trade association first. Such rewards are not considered to be remuneration and are solely at the discretion of the organization.

Reward choices for engagement

So, having established that non-cash is more effective/motivational as a reward to change behaviour than cash, what type of non-cash rewards would be suitable for engagement programmes and how much should you offer?

When it comes to choosing which rewards to offer, there will be national differences mainly due to culture and ease of local redemption. Values may change depending on local average remuneration scales. Table 11.1 shows the hierarchy of rewards choice that is deemed to be true with almost any sample. We have already discussed the fact that although most research participants claim that cash is their preferred reward they actually improve their performance more with non-cash incentives. Ignoring cash for now, overseas travel (hosted group or individual) normally comes out on top, followed by retail cards or credits, specific merchandise, then domestic hotel breaks and finally tickets for sporting events. It is curious that tickets for

TABLE 11.1   Reward types – percentage of companies using them

Reward type	Percentage
Cash	43
Overseas travel	35
Gift cards	23
Merchandise/tangibles	20
Hotel weekends	16
Sports events	14

SOURCE: Fisher, 2008

sporting events ranks so low in the table. When questioned, many 'winners' of invitations to sporting events say that they can recall attending the particular event but could not remember who sponsored it or why they had qualified to receive the tickets. If the purpose of recognition is to reinforce desired performance then a reward where 'winners' cannot remember what it was for is not very effective.

As with most reward decisions the next task is to determine how much is appropriate for what type of performance. The reward choice is determined by what the ROI is for any specific incentive or recognition activity for a particular audience. Let's look at the top of the tree in terms of incentive programmes... travel rewards.

Channel sales incentives

Getting attention for the channel requires investment. Despite the fact that they may have a volume-related contract with you as a supplier, your field team still needs to work very hard to establish cordial business relationships on a one-to-one basis. If there is competition for share of their working day, one of the remedies is to run tactical promotions to attract the sellers' attention to your product.

We have mentioned spiffs in Chapter 8 – they are usually one-day promotional activities conducted on the sales floor offering low-level incentives for specifying manufacturer sales. On a more strategic level, any channel strategy should include tactical promotional periods that last from one to three months with a group travel incentive for the top achievers, following the rewards hierarchy above. Typically this would be promoted through a bespoke incentive website with leader boards showing who is on track to qualify for the travel incentive, along with other colleagues or indeed top achievers from other distribution organizations. The travel incentive would be hosted by the manufacturer who will use it as an opportunity to get to know the best indirect sellers and encourage them to become more engaged in what the manufacturer is trying to achieve commercially.

Travel is the most expensive reward but everything is relative to the ROI you are hoping to achieve. A hosted group of incentive winners could cost tens of thousands, not to mention the cost of setting up the website and ongoing promotion to encourage sellers to qualify.

Employed salespeople incentives

Sales incentives and conventions for employees have a long history and have enabled an entire performance improvement industry to grow up in many parts of the world. In the past many hotel groups have staked their commercial futures on attracting 'incentive groups' into their properties during shoulder periods to augment their revenues. Incentive guests tend to spend much more than individual holidaymakers and often eat in the hotel rather than outside. In the 1970s and 1980s the incentive travel market was dominated by automotive, financial services and pharmaceutical groups travelling the world in their hundreds, staying in luxury properties and enjoying biblical-style gala dinners to recognize top performers. But fashions change, economies are cyclical and those days are long gone; organizations are downsizing in other sections and all costs come under scrutiny. But they can be very effective, when constructed well and targeted at the best performers.

It's a simple marketing proposition. Spend 100,000, get 120,000 back in profits and provide reasons for your top performing sales people to stay with you. Any VP who assesses an advertising budget will recognize the process. As we have seen from Table 11.1, travel works best in terms of attractiveness and performance improvement, so a travel trip is what is offered as the incentive. In broad terms some 5 per cent of the sales force will qualify but their combined incremental revenue could well represent some 50 per cent of total sales in many industries, so well worth the wager.

Of course the activity itself needs to be acceptable to the other employees, following the strategic brand engagement principle of inclusiveness and collaboration. For these reasons incentives now tend to include a learning development element or some kind of thought leadership so that the time spent as a group is taken full advantage of. In many cases there are representatives from the support and administration teams who also attend as they have helped the best sellers achieve their goals by dealing with the paperwork – where 'the sale' is a combination of many people's efforts it is only logical to include others from the team who have contributed to the success. Typically this will be in software development or professional services.

It has to be said that the intangible benefits of gathering together your best, most engaged people to socialize are often unquantifiable in corporate life but can be a great source of future success. Simply knowing the person who performs a particular technical function could be pivotal in the next big tender. Employees in different silos rarely meet up and talk to each other and opportunities to do so can only be beneficial.

Employee engagement incentives

Rewards need to be appropriate to lifestyles as well as being effective. For channel sellers, there is an expectation that above-average sales will be well rewarded and many programmes are set up on the basis of, say, 10 per cent of the average seller's remuneration for that period being a big enough carrot to grab their attention. They have a high risk, often insecure job which they could possibly lose if they underperform.

For employees, the expectation is somewhat different. They have relatively secure contracts and are measured over a longer period with more rounded performance outcomes. As business is all about the careful use of scarce resources, the types and the values of incentives for employees are more constrained. It would be hard to justify, commercially, the rewarding of high-performing employees with lavish trips overseas for simply doing what you ask or complying with some new process. The measurement criteria for success are somewhat less obvious than for sales, so deciding who should get 'the big prize' is often unsatisfactory. The organization would soon be bankrupt if it rewarded all employees for compliance, however desired that outcome may be. A more subtle approach for employees is often taken.

Incentives to conduct your job role tend to be more token than actual, with more emphasis on public recognition of a job well done rather than the intrinsic value of any reward attached to the behaviour. For this reason there may well be individual (rather than hosted group) holidays or even time-off credits for the very best performers, with most 'winners' receiving gift cards or credits at a much lower level than would be normal for sales-people, say 1 or 2 per cent of the appropriate remuneration for that period. Specific merchandise may be a good option for employee programmes as attractive discounts can be negotiated for bulk item orders, way below normal retail prices. The benefit is that the rewards may be perceived to be of a higher value than they actually are, and certainly better than the equivalent in gift cards.

There is also an employee mindset that is not used to being 'incentivized' in the same way as salespeople and in many organizations an over-the-top, promotionally strong programme may not fit with the values of career-minded professionals who may be happy to be recognized by their peers but would feel uncomfortable with receiving excessive rewards for simply 'doing their job'.

Recognition programmes

There should be no reward without recognition and no recognition without reward. If you reward with no peer group recognition you have wasted most of the benefit as an engagement initiative: the point about recognition is to show others the role models and 'ambassadors' in the organization... and for you the organizer to take the credit. If you recognize employees without reward of some kind, however small, you risk being perceived as mean and penny-pinching. After all, how much does it cost to produce a paper certificate? Digital certificates and 'well done' notes cost almost nothing to produce and most employees know that.

There are a number of standard recognition programme formats that can play a crucial background role in supporting strategic brand engagement. They are mostly appropriate for employees but they could be adapted for the channel and advocates with some changes in tone of voice and reward value.

Peer group recognition programmes

In large organizations where success depends on lots of interaction between colleagues, both in your own team or across the organization, it makes sense to encourage collaborative activity. In addition it is often hard to focus employee attention on the main goals and values of the organization when process tasks take up so much time and energy. In the rush to achieve short-term project goals, the main aspirations and values of the organization can get forgotten. In former times re-aligning employees around the values and objectives would normally be done at annual employee meetings or team briefings; the internet has made such refocusing much easier.

The process is as follows. The brand engagement strategy will have clarified the core values of the organization, typically four or five key elements. The idea is to publicly recognize and reward, at a token level, any activity that supports these core values. All employees would visit an intranet website, which is secured by a password in the normal way for internal sites. The programme invites them to 'vote for' or nominate, say, five individuals a month who demonstrate the organization's core values at floor level. The system would normally provide access to an all-employee database so that an employee can easily search for the person to be nominated together with their section (there may be more than one person with the same name). The core values are also shown and nominators simply indicate which value they want to nominate the nominee for. Over time the nominations build up and leading nominees emerge. At the end of the year or other chosen time period the top nominees are then recognized publicly through presentations and rewarded through prizes, if appropriate.

During the programme the system can be written in such a way that a simple 'thank you' can be sent to anyone in the system for positive collaboration, whether or not they represent specific core values. (You can also send birthday wishes or special occasion messages.) As all activity and data can be linked to Google Analytics or similar database analysis programs, managers and the programme administrators can see who has done what and when. This enables the programme to be actively managed across the organization with real-time reports on what values are being nominated, what the most engaged areas are and, equally important, which managers are not using the programme. It may be, for example, that poor customer service scores are concentrated within specific work groups and those work groups are not using the recognition system, suggesting some systemic managerial action needs to be taken to reengage with those groups.

Peer group recognition also works for teams as the employee database could be formulated in such a way as to be able to create an informal working group like a pitch project team or the office move team. In this way recognizing collaboration above and beyond individual efforts can be included in the system.

Ideas programmes

Ideas or suggestion schemes have been in existence for over 130 years. William Denny of the William Denny Ship Building Company of Dumbarton, Glasgow set up his pioneering system 'Rules for the Awards Committee to guide them in rewarding the workmen for inventions and improvements' in 1871. This was the world's first attempt to systematically solicit suggestions from employees and to promote creativity in a company. Other claims to be the first include the Krupp Steel Works in Germany and NCR in the United States.

Although some 40 per cent of organizations claim to have formal or informal systems for employees to offer improvement ideas, in the latter part of the 20th century most programmes fell into disrepute, either through poor management or simply ineffective promotion. The internet has changed all that. In the same way that peer group recognition programmes now provide an instant, relatively admin-free way to recognize extraordinary performance, ideas can now be collected, analyzed, refined and implemented much more easily via intranet systems.

Employees are enrolled in the ideas scheme online, automatically. The programme is promoted as an engagement tool to encourage two types of idea:

- ways to generate revenue/create organizational benefits; and
- ways to reduce costs.

Challenging participants to concentrate on these two categories eliminates some 90 per cent of 'old-system' suggestions that tended to block up the assessment process and cause delays in rewarding good suggestions and recognizing individual contributions. When ideas are submitted online you can include checks and balances to ensure that only relevant ideas go into the assessment process through FAQs (Frequently Asked Questions) that offer advice about what a good idea looks like, and through team manager approvals before ideas are sent through.

CASE STUDY   ME

Lucent Technologies introduced an ideas programme called 'It's All About ME', specifically for employees of its Micro Electronics division. They could earn points by submitting cost-saving or revenue-generating ideas that could be redeemed for merchandise and other rewards through a catalogue. The set up and promotion of the programme was entirely covered by the savings made. Over 54 per cent of employees participated (you might expect around 25 per cent to participate in general, depending on the level of promotion) who provided over 6,000 ideas, of which 2,100 were 'implemented' in one form or another. Examples included recycling scrap, reducing the cost of overnight deliveries and making e-mail more efficient. The net benefit to the division was $20 million in the first year.

Ideas schemes mostly justify their existence by being able to allocate true cost savings/additional revenues that would not have happened otherwise. Experience shows that as such programmes become part of the organizational wallpaper their effectiveness fades away and they are either simply tolerated or abandoned completely. With good communication and alignment with ever-changing corporate objectives and values there is no reason why such programmes cannot be revamped every two or three years to provide net benefits for many years. Schneider Electric has a current employee communication/recognition programme called 'Connect', which was deliberately created to run for three years only with the aim of rebranding and reinvigorating it once the three years ends. This is a sensible approach as it forces those responsible to review what they are doing and spending in terms of effectiveness and relevance.

Hybrid recognition programmes

One of the benefits of internet and wireless technology is the facility to create new ways to communicate and recognize employees at minimum cost. So, rather than have designated programmes for peer group recognition and ideas collection, it is perfectly possible to combine the two initiatives under one system/brand and offer core values recognition *and* ideas generation in one programme. Taking this idea further, the web system could be adapted for mobiles to enable those who work off site or globally to take part in the programme as well. Thanks to improvements in applications technology anyone with a tablet or mobile phone can be as easily connected to the centre as those who work from desktop systems. This is already available for expenses payment systems and reports access, so why not employee recognition systems and suggestion schemes?

'Employee of the month'

Wherever you go in the world, there will always be a small poster in a supermarket or automotive repair facility which shows this month's 'best employee'. Many are poorly produced, somewhat faded by sunlight, with pictures that look as if they were taken in a correctional institution. Often the same employee's name crops up in the list of previous best performers. Quite often the poster is several months out of date. And when someone leaves, blank spaces appear where there should be a face. Not very encouraging for first-time customers or new recruits visiting your place of work.

If something is easy to produce, it does not follow that you should simply do it and claim that you have ticked that particular recognition box. Such paying of lip-service to the theory and practice of employee recognition does more harm than good to your brand. Rather than enhance what should be a positive communication it makes the organization look amateurish, lacking in follow-through and uncaring. It would be better to show nothing than to harm the brand by defective execution of what should be a beneficial message.

The principle here is that all reward and recognition initiatives need to be updated and examined critically on a regular basis to see how they align with your core values. If 'employee of the month' comes across as outdated, no longer in fashion and possibly a bit of a joke, stop doing it. There are many other online and interpersonal ways to recognize good performance. In the age of the tablet and mobile communication, perhaps taking such promotion wireless should be considered. Taking it out of the public domain and making it more individual to employees reflects the way people expect to be treated these days, not to mention issues to do with personal data protection in the workplace. If you have to ask permission to publicly recognize good performance, maybe your recognition system needs a fundamental overhauling.

Advocate recognition and ideas generation

Advocates and unpaid ambassadors have a special place in any rewards system you may wish to implement. They do not do what they do for the reward element, by definition. But recognition and token rewards are effective reinforcers, so they should be part of your strategic engagement plan. Because advocates and ambassadors have no direct vested interest in the process improvements they are often well-placed to spot inefficiencies or errors in their interaction with the organization. You need to think about ways for them to contribute, above and beyond their voluntary efforts.

Saying thanks is a good basis for involving advocates in the ongoing engagement process. Ways to do this include inviting them to 'meet the team' a few times a year for a lunch and discussion about how the organization can help them do more advocacy. You could enrol them in your ideas programme as they may have some useful external views on how you could interact with them and improve your service. You may feel it useful to create 'annual awards' to recognize their contribution with peer recognition certificates and some kind of ceremony. A video of their activities, as part of your CSR programme may be appropriate when reporting back what they do at employee briefings or town hall meetings. Depending on what your product or service is, you could lend them products so that they can demonstrate them to friends and colleagues at appropriate times. There is no reason why they cannot be part of the process of recruiting new employees, with token rewards for successfully introducing new people to the organization.

Town hall meetings and social events

In recent years there has been much emphasis placed on justifying large, discretional expenditures and employee meetings have come under scrutiny simply because the cost of hosting an event for, say, 500 employees is not small. Organizations should look at the strategic brand engagement plan for employees and check that there are enough touch points for recognition and feedback before cancelling events. If structured correctly in terms of the exchange of information and the opportunities to make contributions off site, events are often eagerly anticipated by employees and seen as being worth attending and enjoyable. In this way loyalty is enhanced and employees feel they are valued and their opinions are taken into consideration.

Social programmes are often the poor relation of engagement programmes and overlooked as an important medium for promoting loyalty and broad engagement. In many organizations employees will form their own social programmes and often pay for all the costs themselves. Christmas lunches, Friday drinks after work or summer barbecues all form part of the informal matrix that binds organizations together and it is always in the interests of the organization to facilitate such events even if they do not contribute any budget.

Creating mutual respect

Non-cash incentives, token rewards and recognition systems for employees, the channel and advocates come and go at an alarming rate, leaving many organizations with a triage job to do on the 'walking wounded' of what remains. While many thousands are spent on consultancy advice to establish market fit for remuneration and bonuses, the most efficient ways to recruit and retain people to support your brand get neglected. When a recognition programme falls into disrepair it creates more reasons for the uninterested to remain disengaged and for the engaged to wonder if they made the right decision to 'stick with it' when that well-known competitor came up with that improved job offer last week. To get things working well again, discretional reward and recognition programmes need to be dusted off, checked for fitness of purpose and rebranded in line with current strategies. Doing this every year, with a major rethink every three years, will enhance your reputation in the marketplace and maintain strong levels of engagement, which is the entire and only purpose of such internal programmes.

Replacing employees who leave remains a key task for any employer. Consultants often talk about 'the employer brand' and how this helps to attract new employees or put them off before they even apply for a position. In the following chapter we look at what employer brands look like and how they should be part of the bigger brand engagement strategy.

Recruitment and the employer brand

12

> *The first point to realise is that you already have one [a recruitment brand]. That doesn't mean someone in HR went out and developed it. It simply means that your organization has a reputation as a place to work.*
>
> **(CHARTERED INSTITUTE OF PERSONNEL AND DEVELOPMENT, 2012)**

In Chapter 3 we explored the idea that all active organizations already have a brand, whether they are positively promoted or not. The same is true of their employer brand when it comes to recruiting new employees, promoting to channel partners and offering advocacy opportunities. When thinking about strategic brand engagement one of the most powerful tools in your promotional box is how you use your employer brand to engage with potential employees who, as yet, do not work for you. It also allows you to promote to an audience who are already employees and may well be consumers or advocates for you, because employees also look at your job advertisements. With such a broad opportunity to get people engaging with your brand it makes sense that it should at least be consistent with the master consumer brand.

Recruitment advertising is still advertising, a paid-for communication, so it should support the values of the master brand and to reinforce the brand through professional communication and logical, promotional planning to engage consumers, potential employees and existing employees in your organization. There are some excellent examples of integrating the master brand and the recruitment brand from many industry sectors... but there are many more that simply pay lip-service to branding. At the heart of the problem lies the issue of HR experts trying to be marketing experts and marketing experts trying to be HR experts. In *Living the Brand*, Nicholas Ind, a Scandinavian brand consultant, neatly sums up this point when talking about recruitment advertising:

> This ought to be an opportunity to make a statement about the brand... The disconnection between human resources and marketing means that companies do not seize the opportunity... Either the opportunity is missed and/or there are large doses of dissonance. (Ind, 2012)

Recruitment branding offers the ideal common ground where HR and marketing can come together and pursue the same engagement objectives. But if you do align your recruitment advertising with your brand, will it actually work better? ROI is the acid test.

In 2005 The Bernard Hodes Group conducted a survey of HR professionals around the world about whether an integrated employer brand improves the quality of actual replies. Eighty-one per cent said it did, 51 per cent said it resulted in a shorter recruitment tail between applications and accepted offers and 44 per cent claimed it produced a higher acceptance rate. A reader survey in the UK HR magazine *Personnel Today* in the same period put employer branding as an important or very important issue for 79 per cent of HR senior managers (Willock, 2005). So, overall, well over half of HR professionals thought there were benefits in branding recruitment efforts in an integrated way rather than booking the media space and pasting in a logo in the bottom corner. Recruitment costs continue to be a key issue for many organizations, so making essential advertising more effective, especially on-line where the majority of recruitment activity now happens, will continue to be an organizational priority.

A 'Great Place to Work'

In Chapter 7 we discussed marketing the brand internally. When it comes to recruitment advertising the core values of the organization will be projected beyond the confines of your offices and the intranet and out into the wider world. The impact of social media and its speed means that recruitment advertising needs to reflect the core values and brand image of your mainstream marketing as it is now, not as it was the last time you advertised, which could have been a year ago or more. If the headline jars or the logo is wrong, it tells the world that the organization is unregulated and does not really believe in a consistent brand image and, by extension, nor does it believe in consistency in dealing with people and business planning. So, not such a great place to work after all. The result is fewer applications and possibly online ridicule from a very savvy and unforgiving pool of new talent who are comfortable with social media and know how to publish examples of lack of professionalism.

The building blocks of brand-consistent recruitment advertising are, therefore, as follows:

- Revisit the core brand values and check they are still true/not undergoing a major revision.
- Check core brand imagery, logos, typefaces, local usage, the brand book requirements and other technical production issues.
- Review internal research on employee perceptions of the brand and consumer research about the brand to look for consistencies and alignments. If there are perception gaps, understand why.
- Take note of the main benefits of why employees like working for you and decide what to feature: they could be physical such as 'nice offices' or they could be aspirational such as 'market leader' or 'innovative'.
- Find compelling reasons as to why they should work for you, sometimes known as employee value propositions (EVPs).
- Is there a 'big idea' that could be a market differentiator for a particular role?

If the marketing people have done their job effectively the organization will already have a clear, core values proposition, so read up on it and think how that plays out within the current parts of the business for recruitment purposes. From time to time there will be revisions to the values such as when a new, major target is acquired or a new CEO joins the senior team. The gestation period for changes to core values could be months or years depending on the size of the organization, so it may be 'business as usual' when it comes to branding until a formal announcement is made. But be careful about ongoing recruitment arrangements with all your media. They may not be aware that things may be changing and that they will need new materials to work with if a major change announcement is made.

For international organizations there will be a need to remain flexible to local needs, so creating recruitment brand imagery that works in global markets is a challenge. If local languages are used with local key words and cultural values the branding may need to be blander than the marketers would prefer and in keeping with local competitors. It may well be that you can outspend your local rivals in terms of positioning within media and with the professionalism of the imagery, but take care that this 'differentiator' does not put candidates off. Empathy rather than superiority should be the creative watchword. All marketing needs to appeal to its audience in a positive way. 'Glocalization' is still an important marketing principle, even at the expense of the brand book, if the guidelines clearly make no sense in your specific corner of the world. If there is a unique event happening (the Olympics, for example) or there is an ongoing media story everyone is aware of, consider whether being topical may help your recruitment advertisement stand out.

One of the most striking mismatches for any employee is that between consumer marketing and the employer brand. International hotel brands, for example, are keenly targeted to wealthy market segments with all the peripheral imagery of conspicuous consumption and the enjoyment of leisure or business travel relaxation. Most hotel employees are on minimum wage and are some of the lowest paid workers in many parts of the world. When considering the recruitment brand, attention needs to be paid to this gap so that potential employees are not 'sold' a proposition that is untrue. As in all marketing 'cognitive dissonance' – the feeling that something does not match expectations after purchase – needs to be avoided if the hire is to be successful. So, rather than promoting the luxury attributes of the product a hotelier recruiting new staff may emphasize a 'caring employer' or the security of employment, for example, to ensure that recruits get what they expect from their employment. For example, a strapline such as 'Where everyone matters' could work well across all brands, including the recruitment brand, as a statement of a positive corporate value.

Employee value propositions

EVPs are what drive the details of the offer and the main reason why a candidate may become a recruit. It goes without saying that the propositions would reflect the main brand, but different sectors and departments have different needs for recruiting. So each major employing group needs to work out what the main drivers would be for recruits to their particular part of the organization. If it is a sales job there may be an emphasis on achievement of personal goals, better lifestyle, etc. If it is a technical position you may want to emphasize the chance to be part of a ground-breaking team or helping to develop unique and innovative products. These differences in EVP could have their own strapline that complements the main brand but brings out the importance of a key factor in the job which you believe will appeal to more candidates.

CASE STUDY GE

The General Electric main website is globally branded 'imagination at work'. For each recruiting division there is a personal profile of a real employee with a brief phrase that embodies a value-based description of what working for GE in that particular division is like. In GE Sensory, for example, 'Steve Chalmers' is a production sales inventory leader but his description of his own job is values-based and aspirational: 'We lead youths through a series of workshops to get them to think, dream and create the vision of what the future may hold for them.'

You can see here that the master brand strapline – imagination at work – has been echoed in the statement, using words like 'dream' and 'vision' to create a description of a development job that has wider meaning than simply delivering training courses.

Promotional aspects

If you apply marketing principles to recruitment advertising you may find the differentiator for success that all advertisers look for. Marketers refer to this as 'the big idea'. What could be different about your recruitment advertising in a crowded market where everyone appears to be chasing the same candidates?

Using the four Ps you could begin your internal debate by knowing where you fit in the average rate of pay for similar employers and whether your benefits are still perceived as valuable (price) and take a view on whether you could afford to offer more to outdo your rivals. You could examine where you traditionally place adverts or announcements and think about other distribution routes such as social media (place). You could repackage the role to see if by adding other elements the role may appeal to a wider candidate pool (product). Finally, you could think through the cost advantages of dealing through one agency or one medium to get priority over other advertisers, or do an experiential event at a trade fair to gather new names (promotion). Any or all of these aspects of the four Ps could result in the 'big idea' that you need to differentiate your offer from all the others in the market.

Social networking

As we have already discovered, social media is a new route to market for which hard and fast rules are still being worked out when it comes to recruiting good calibre candidates. Although printed media are still popular for key national positions in the public sector, aimed at Baby Boomers in the main, middle-level positions aimed at Generation Y may be better placed in social media with a business bias. The statistics show that online promotion and applications may well be the default method to find out about new positions and to go through the early stages of candidate selection that lead to the shortlist.

Those people looking for a new position are likely to be using Facebook, Twitter or LinkedIn for other social contacts during any working day so it is an obvious place to have a recruitment brand presence. Twitter has 900 million accounts and Facebook has over 1 billion members (May 2013) so they are hard to ignore as a place to 'meet' new employees.

Facebook

Some analysts have pointed out that Facebook members, globally, spend on average some 400 minutes per month on the site, which is equivalent to around 20 minutes per working day. Your corporate Facebook site should therefore carry a careers tab so that jobseekers can easily find any current opportunities while they are browsing the site. You can update, remove and amend any details of the positions on a live basis by linking the page to your core recruiting platform, so candidates who have liked the page can apply for any position without leaving the Facebook page.

Your Facebook page should provide a true picture of your organization and its outlook, and leave a fresh impression in the minds of candidates as to what you are all about and your attitudes to the issues of the day, and demonstrate how you, as an organization, deal with the world at large. You can start discussions on general employment topics or newsy items relating to the jobs market or your industry without having to oversell the organization and, once members get involved in the dialogue, they are just one click away from making an application. By enabling engagement in a positive way candidates will come to you rather than you having to fund advertising or engage agencies to find them for you. Facebook is an open channel in recruitment terms so apply your brand consistently so that candidates move seamlessly from your Facebook page to your other sites.

Twitter

As outlined in Chapter 10, you need to do some listening first on Twitter to identify who is talking about what within your job role target markets. Analyse what hash tags and keywords they are using. When you have a clear picture of industry-specific chats you can tag any available positions to likely candidates. One important metric is to discover what time of day or day of the week they tend to tweet on. This enables you to tweet just at the time they are likely to be engaging in job-related chat. The key to Twitter is to be friendly, useful and engaging, providing a genuine benefit to a chat group. Once a following is established you can then consider what positions may be relevant and how to introduce the offer, in the same way that you would if you met someone in a social situation.

LinkedIn

LinkedIn is the world's largest network of professional people, with 160 million professional profiles, making it ideal for finding qualified recruits. Interaction is centred on forums and industry-specific online groups so the strategy would be to encourage likely candidates to join the forum groups to which you regularly contribute. Things to post would be requests for help and information, views on a current industry issue, management techniques or recommended suppliers. The aim would be for contributors to be on your LinkedIn page with direct links to your corporate site/recruitment page. One of the often forgotten benefits of LinkedIn is that many of your existing employees will already be members, so using their contacts and activities would help to direct potential candidates to your job opportunities through comment and suggestions.

Keep engaged

Depending on your industry sector there may be many other sites where creating a group or getting involved with live discussions or exchange of images can only be beneficial, such as Pinterest. Google+ also provides the opportunity to link with anyone, not just those in your Facebook or LinkedIn groups, which means you can add new candidates to an ever-widening circle.

In all these social media opportunities the tone and style of the interaction needs to be authentic, helpful, interesting and sociable rather than corporate. It is a different way to look at marketing and needs to be learnt and then tried out. Simply sending out traditional marketing 'push' messages will backfire badly so as in all social exchanges the needs of the other party should come first in order to reap the eventual rewards of being part of a group that has mutual respect.

A word of caution. Social media is not a panacea for complete recruitment success and brand engagement harmony. Other media and selection processes still need to be in the mix and just as organizations put on a public face in public places so do individuals. Charlie Griffiths of Stonor Recruitment, a UK-based consultancy comments:

> The danger of relying on social media to gauge someone's background, personality and suitability is that often it's an online 'mask' of how they want to be perceived. Meeting someone face-to-face will often give a much better understanding of their capabilities when recruiting. On the flip-side the internet is a great resource for finding information on candidates. There is also the risk of missing out on more discerning candidates who do not want their career details splattered all over the internet!
>
> (Private communication)

As in all searches for the most effective solution at the lowest cost, putting all your eggs in one solutions basket is never a good idea. The strategic brand engagement story as applied to recruitment is to be consistent and not allow the master brand to be damaged by different sets of core values and imagery. There has to be a continuous and consistent thread for the cumulative effect of a common brand.

For brand engagement to be effective it has to tally with all your other pronouncements in the public media and be perceived to be sincere and supporting your core values. Recruitment advertising and activities are arguably one of the most important of all the marketing dialogues as one slip of the tongue could ruin an organization's public profile for many years. If you amplify a mistake many millions of times in a short period, which is what social media are good at, you need to have the resources and the courage to say sorry and undo it quickly or suffer the consequences. The tone and style of social media present many challenges in that the natural communication environment is informal and conversational and often unchecked by any central authority. This approach may be diametrically opposed to normal public brand marketing. So remaining engaged within the confines of new social media norms is a balancing act for which there are, as yet, few written rules.

Things do not always go according to plan, of course. However much planning you do and advice you take there is always going to be a certain percentage of any audience or employee group that will not respond. Should we just accept this or are there actions we can take to mitigate the effects of the world not being perfect? In the next chapter we examine the effects of disengagement and what remedies are available to put things right.

Dealing with disengagement

13

> *Looking across a number of major industry sectors, between 32 and 48 per cent of employees report work conditions that do not allow them to be as productive as they could be.*
>
> **(HAY GROUP AUSTRALIA, 2012)**

It is relatively easy to show what improvements were achieved as a result of any engagement programme you may have implemented – benchmarking and research are part of the process. But it is less straightforward to calculate the specific, detrimental effects of not addressing such issues in any organization. Sector statistics are one thing, but what is actually happening in your own corporation is unique and hard to assess. What we can see, though, are the symptoms of doing nothing about fostering positive engagement.

Some commentators prefer to use the term 'passively disinterested' rather than disengaged. In a study conducted by the Entec Corporation in 2012 the disinterested were described as follows:

> It means they come to work, they do what they are asked to do and they will not do more than required. They will not make suggestions for improving processes or work methods in their departments. They will not offer up any new ideas. They are not emotionally involved. They do their work and when the day ends they leave punctually. They don't think about their work or their organizations after they leave.
>
> (Entec Corporation, 2012)

These employees are not necessarily doing a bad job and to some extent their work patterns are hard to change. The real challenge is to address the 'actively disengaged' (the figure ranges from 5 to over 40 per cent in extreme cases) who make no effort to be cooperative and infect other employees with their negative activities. In practical terms, disengagement means processes getting done at minimum quality levels, employees withdrawing from voluntary action, difficulties with recruitment and retention, lack of interdepartmental cooperation, a 'no-can-do' attitude.

We have shown in Chapter 1 why positive engagement matters to organizations in general. But what are the signs of strategic brand disengagement in individual organizations and how many signs do you need to see before you have to take positive action and address the issue in a joined-up way?

Disengagement and disinterest among employees

Disengagement can manifest itself in several ways. As usual, you need to distinguish between a one-off aberration and a long-term pattern. But even at a subliminal level most employees 'know' that something is wrong long before it gets on the senior management agenda. In this chapter we will walk through the most common causes of organizational disengagement, which range from performance management, communication issues, work structures and empowerment through to personal development and even the everyday tasks themselves. According to Gallup Organization research as far back as 2002 up to 55 per cent of US employees are 'not engaged' in their jobs: 'These employees are essentially "checked out". They're sleepwalking through their workday, putting in time – but not energy or passion – into their work.'

The remedy may be to take some action with specific individuals. But if it is systemic response to the workplace – almost everyone seems to behave this way – and the organization is actively provoking disengagement, possibly without realizing it, then a more strategic brand engagement programme will be required. But even if your aggregate scores on engagement are good, you may still need to take action. In an article in Gallup's *Business Journal* in 2004, Glenn Phelps warned against complacency, even if your overall engagement scores are relatively favourable:

When assessing how engaged your employees are, looking at company-wide data can be revealing – and comforting too, if the numbers look good. But executives beware. It's easy to draw the wrong conclusions from a series of consistently high overall company engagement scores. Your company's overall score may be stable and high, but that doesn't mean the work environment is uniformly productive. If the interactions in a given workgroup are more negative than positive, that group may produce a pocket of 'disengaged workers' who are profoundly disconnected from their work – and those workers may be costing your company a lot of money.

(Phelps, 2004)

Lack of performance feedback

There is an apocryphal story about the famous Hollywood actor who says in a media interview, 'Well, that's enough about me, what did *you* think of my performance?' It is human nature to look for approval and feedback on performance of all kinds, so it is no surprise that when people do not get regular or indeed any feedback on performance at work, their personal motivation dips and disaffection grows. A number of studies over the years have found that up to 40 per cent of employees do not receive formal appraisals or have any mechanism for feedback from their managers.

This works both ways. Employees never find out if what they are doing is beneficial for the organization. Managers have no opportunity to set out clear objectives, either for the individual or for the organization as a whole. In a mature corporation with products everyone knows well, such as automotive, managers may consider it obvious what is expected and by when. But young people joining the workforce, for example, may not be aware that there are processes to complete and deadlines to hit. New recruits may have come from an employment background with no specific commercial goals other than 'to do as much as you can'. So unless they are told what is required, it would be hard for them to guess what the performance standards actually are.

The entire process of human resources good practice in job specification, job descriptions, probationary periods, interim reviews and career development are all very well, but if a divisional leader or work unit manager undermines the process by not complying with it, then employees suffer. Non-compliance is not just a tick-box exercise. By their general attitude and the way they respond to human resources requests when they think no one in the hierarchy is watching, disengaged managers spread their disaffection to their teams in many subtle ways.

Feedback and appraisals should not just happen once a year 'with witnesses'. There should be informal mechanisms throughout the year in the form of one-to-one briefings, post-project round-ups and new project discussions so that dealing with change at work becomes an ongoing and natural process, not just something imposed on team leaders from the organizational hub as an annoying and time-consuming compliance issue.

Lack of empowerment

A common complaint from employees within 'disengaged' organizations is the lack of empowerment. In many instances employees are given the responsibility to achieve specific tasks but are then disciplined informally for trying to achieve them. It may be that the manager has not fully explained the consequences of over-reaching levels of authority – there may be financial reasons – but in general employees will revert to 'staying in the box' if their genuine urge to achieve more is stifled by regular put-downs. In these work environments productivity is measurably less than in comparable units/divisions, even with the same resources, so it is relatively easy to spot as an engagement issue. The numbers rarely lie.

In some cases it is the team leader over-reacting to orders from his or her own line manager that causes the issue. Senior VPs may be desperate for their supervisors to take more control of the day-to-day decisions to free themselves up to do broader projects. But unwittingly they may be promoting the culture of 'don't go out on a limb' by asking for too many performance reports, too frequently. If employees are encouraged to 'think for themselves' but are monitored remotely through reports and e-mail traffic on a daily basis then most will decline or delay implementing any different or new ideas.

Typically disengaged employees do not volunteer for development or further skills training because they claim they cannot miss out on providing what they perceive to be 'key data reports' to their line managers. For empowerment and delegation to work, the hand of management needs to rest lightly on the steering wheel and team members need to feel they have permission to deviate from the routine from time to time if there is a bigger benefit that could be gained from doing so.

Lack of resources

Stress at work is closely related to the amount of control individuals have over their workload and the timely organization of their daily tasks. Deadlines, overwork and lack of relevant resources are the enemies of positive engagement. At least a third of employees complain in surveys that their organization does not provide the manpower needed at all times to complete tasks, or that the information they need to do their job is inadequate or simply not provided in an appropriate format. The consequence of not having enough resources is that employees stop suggesting innovations and accept the reality of too much work and not enough time to do it in.

Late with replacements

An often hidden disengagement factor that falls within this category is the tendency for many organizations, big and small, not to replace employees in a timely fashion when someone leaves or is let go. From the organization's viewpoint the longer it takes to replace someone the less cost there appears to be, and invariably the slack is taken up by other employees in the same section because collectively they need to accomplish the tasks as a group. But it is a short-sighted way of managing employees. Those who have to fill the gap resent the extra effort they have to put in to cover for the missing employees and goodwill is soon eroded if there is no replacement on the way. It may also be that senior VPs have decided that they must try to reduce headcount anyway, so there is pressure on HR to 'take their time' when replacing employees in the belief that the costs of replacement and training are spread out over a longer period.

Lack of personal development

Although many organizations say they offer personal development on a regular basis as part of their people development policy, development budgets are often unspent and it is difficult to persuade managers that their teams need to acquire new skills, however long they may have been employed. This is partly due to the work pressure syndrome as described above: employees feel they cannot take 'time out' when their friends and colleagues are under pressure. It also suits many team leaders not to follow through with skills development offers as they too are under pressure from the management team above them to deliver processes on time and to an agreed standard, even though they know they may be under-resourced.

Investing in the future can be a difficult message to sell when everyone is under pressure to deliver.

In some circumstances offers to learn new skills are not taken up by long-term employees as they feel that they have already found ways around a lack of skills over the years with 'make-do-and-mend' procedures. Often the person or group that had the necessary skills for a specific task has moved on and not been replaced and, unknown to the manager, the team has found a way to replicate the old skill but in a less efficient way. The fact that things still appear to run smoothly makes the case for retraining less obvious. As for the employees, they feel there is nothing that can be done and they simply have to add it to the list of stresses and pressures to accomplish ever more tasks with diminishing resources.

Lack of collaboration

In small organizations it is normal to find people to rally around the corporate flag and perhaps take on tasks that strictly speaking they are not formally employed to do. As organizations get bigger, tasks are demarcated, job descriptions and rates of pay are formalized and employees tend to follow a predictable pattern of what they will and will not do as part of their 'contract' with the employer, however pleasant and positive the corporate ethos is or however strong the pressure is to make an extraordinary effort.

In many large organizations employees feel that they could do a better job if they had more cooperation from other departments, such as finance or, dare we say it, human resources. Sales functions often complain that marketing does not give them the right tools to do their job. Operational areas complain that sales want too many deviations from their standard products and this makes them inefficient. Such 'silo' behaviour needs to be well-managed to achieve the best output from limited overall resources. It's all about compromise and a professional executive will be able to see both sides of the argument and make reasoned judgements as to who should get what and when for any given set of circumstances.

The trouble is employees get caught in the middle and rather than try to deal with the problem, they avoid it by having as little contact as possible with other parts of the organization. This can lead to distrust as to the motives of other departments (they only want that because they get more bonus; they want it by Tuesday because they have been lazy and left it all too late; they provide poor service because they won't spend the budget on qualified people). Sharing of ideas and solutions to common problems is absent from disengaged organizations. Work groups close up and keep themselves to themselves. Eventually this leads to groups working to their own agenda, which may or may not be the agenda of the wider organization.

Lack of structure

Sometimes the fault really does lie in the structure of a work group or even the organization itself. The Volvo 'teamwork' philosophy for automotive production, introduced into a brand new factory in Kalmar, Sweden in 1974, was one of the first manufacturers to recognize that you could achieve higher productivity by getting specialists to work together rather than simply follow Henry Ford's original production model of separate departments adding their contribution in a production line format:

> The Kalmar plant dispensed with Henry Ford's notorious assembly line along which thousands of highly specialized workers perform the same task over and over again as cars or car components move by them at a predetermined speed. The new plant was constructed with many separate rooms, each with a separate entrance and large windows to the world outside. Old union job classifications were abolished, along with the common practice at conventional plants of workers standing idly by while waiting for a fellow worker with the 'proper' classification to perform a narrowly specified task. Instead, all workers were treated as interchangeable, and each room was given to a team of 15 to 25 workers who were made jointly responsible for performing, in a specified time, a broadly defined task, such as electric wiring, door assembly, fitting upholstery, or installing an exhaust system. In each room, there might be 60 different things to do to finish the assigned task, and workers were free to decide how to do it and who did what and when.
>
> (Kohler, 1997)

The main point here is that even with information or software businesses there will be less disengagement if organizations are designed in such a way as to encourage collaboration. With most organizations now benefitting from their own intranets there is no structural reason why collaboration cannot take place at all levels, especially as no one needs to leave their workstation anymore to take advantage of another person's idea.

Disengaged management style

Not all the reasons for disengagement are rooted in the employees' behaviour; sometimes disengagement starts with the management team. As we learnt in Chapter 5, the tone of voice from the very top sets the agenda for the rest of the organization, even very large ones. If senior management are not engaged with each other, it would be unlikely that the rest of the organization would be.

A survey by the UK's Chartered Management Institute in 2012 of 2,000 employees into 'effective management' showed that 75 per cent of employees wasted almost two hours every week as a direct result of poor management/ supervisory practices (CMI, 2012). The instances are not unique to the UK and could probably describe what happens in most large organizations and many small ones all over the world. In general disengaged managers are characterized by the following habits:

- Minimal or misdirected instructions for particular tasks.
- Not available to discuss detail.
- Avoid conflict and difficult people decisions.
- Micro-manage previously delegated tasks.
- Re-work tasks in their own style.
- Think of the political consequences of certain tasks being completed/ not completed.

The result is that most managers under pressure come across to employees as 'self-centred, pessimistic muddlers' who stifle innovation... and worse still, do not see part of their task as fostering engagement in their team or in the enterprise overall. They see this as a 'corporate programme' job which is run by HR and has nothing to do with operational efficiency or people management.

Channel disengagement

If you are in marketing you will have had business experiences with distributors that start off very positively, with strong sales and the development of good personal relationships. Over time the distributors are courted by other suppliers with better financial deals and what is seen as better promotional support. Unless the channel is constantly monitored and communicated with, this route to profits can be easily eroded and much time lost in expensive and time-consuming negotiation to get back on track with the original contract. It may be that your product range is no longer as easy to sell on as before or that your field team has changed and is working on other priorities. Whatever the root cause, channel disengagement can be expensive to fix.

Strategic brand engagement requires that you employ the same engagement techniques for third parties as you would for internal employees, albeit recognizing that they are less likely to comply. It's all about tone of voice and reviewing how the relationship is going.

Improving channel relationships

Regular business reviews with distributor VPs should be held, rather than just annual contract reviews, to ensure that the promises on both sides are being maintained. Part of this process would be a competitive review of new products to ensure you are still able to deliver what the distributors are trying to sell. Regular e-mail research with the actual day-to-day sellers would help to keep track of any dips in sales that cannot be attributed to a dip in the market. Are the field staff doing as many spiffs as they used to (see Chapter 8), what additional permissions need to be sought to keep up the sales pressure, what do the distributor employees think of your quality of representation, especially if it has changed recently?

Another key issue could be that the distributor is consolidating its buying to reduce its own marketing costs and that your organization no longer provides the range of goods and services they require. This may not be obvious until the contract is renewed, so keeping close to existing distributors and, of course, any new distributors is all part of the engagement process. The provision of well-communicated marketing materials could be a key issue as onward sellers need quick and accurate information about your products to pass on to corporate buyers. This may mean a shared portal that is updated to a level that the distributor would expect.

Training may also be an important issue. If your supplier offer depends largely on how your product is used or adapted for use by consumers in various parts of the market you need to update your online and offline training resource so that it better suits the distributors' working day. Traditionally, distributor employees are invited to take part in online product learning sessions in the office or to offsite sessions in local hotels. When times are tough and distributors do not want their employees taking time out of the office and away from their phones, you may need to be more creative about training them. You could consider the idea of branding a truck or mobile exhibition and taking it to their offices as a road show to conduct training in their car park during lunch or immediately after work, thus going that extra mile in getting their employees engaged in your business or organization.

With your key distributors, perhaps not all of them, you often need longer-term engagement than the occasional spif day will allow. With your main distributors, a 'club' format may be appropriate, where the top sellers within your distributors are 'enrolled' in an online club that provides 'membership' benefits, perhaps including privileged product information, a service hotline only available to club members or higher level training than would be provided under the normal contractual terms. With this kind of special assistance, 'disengagement' will be less likely to happen and you, as a supplier, will be able to spot the erosion of engagement more quickly.

Advocate disengagement

Advocates are even less malleable than distributors as their input is purely voluntary. Signs of advocacy disengagement are similar to those for distributors. Ambassador programmes require constant refreshment, promotionally speaking, and perhaps more 'loving care' than even distributors as advocates have no commercial interest in your profits and simply want to represent your interests. The measurements of disengagement would be lower attendance at your events, less online participation in quizzes and training activities, lack of empathy with your values following a new corporate trading stance or a change of leadership, or some bad press as a result of some incident. It may also be that your field team has had a change of emphasis and that for some reason they have withdrawn from advocates in favour of new distributors for commercial reasons.

All are valid commercial reasons to change your marketing emphasis, but once advocates are disengaged it can be very difficult to re-engage them to act for free to the same level as before. So any retreat from dealing with advocates needs to be a conscious, business decision and costed out as 'irreversible' – you can assume it may take years to recover your advocacy support once the ties are broken.

Removing the 'dis' from disengagement

In previous chapters we have seen how to build an engaged organization from the top down and the bottom up. But the vast majority of employees and managers join existing organizations that are already partly engaged and partly disengaged. No consultant would suggest that by following the principles laid out above you will achieve 100 per cent engagement. But once the symptoms of disengagement are spotted you can begin to affect a cure in your own area or section. If you do not have the mandate or the resources to change things root and branch, you could start changing things piecemeal within your own sphere of influence. For example:

- Even if there is an existing annual appraisal system, could you introduce informal, quarterly or even monthly 'reviews' in the form of one-to-ones that concentrate on ideas and suggestions rather than output and performance?

- Create a task briefing list and agree with your team what should be on it to avoid misunderstandings and doing things twice.

- Review the workload as a team and ask employees where the pinch points are and what new resources may be needed to get things done on time.

- If you need to recruit a new team member, get your team to come up with a revised job specification and include any 'soft' tasks that are currently done but not recorded anywhere formally.

- If there is no formal recognition mechanism for going beyond the call of duty, work with your team to create one for them and assign an individual to manage it on a regular basis.

- Reinvent the process for skills development by promoting all the opportunities available and take ownership for using it, asking employees to feed back to the team what they learnt (and perhaps what they didn't).

- Monitor instances of 'disengagement' and allow team members to feed back on why they happened and what could be done to improve things.

- Discuss the relationship your team has with close departments with the aim of reducing silo thinking and better cooperation... sandwiches and an ideas-generation session one lunchtime could set the scene for better cooperation.

- Agree with your supervisory team what positive engagement looks like and work towards changing behaviours bit by bit.

Improving engagement through 'enabling'

In recent years studies have been conducted to show that too much emphasis on leadership rather than people management skills produces less good results. In other words, the tendency to retrain the leaders or change them rarely leads to lasting improvement. That seems pretty obvious. The argument goes that for all the blustering that may go on at the top of the organization if you do not have managers who 'enable' the changes to take place, then the improvements are short-lived – or only as good as the rhetorical skills of a charismatic leader.

Some surveys show that good engagement practices from the top produce two and half times the growth of similar non-engaged organizations but four and a half times the growth if managers are also trained in enablement techniques that coincide with changes at the top. In other words, fine words are great but fine words with practical skills to translate those words into action throughout the entire organization are even better, and tend to last longer.

A balanced scorecard approach

It all comes down to definitions of engagement, disengagement and enablement. The important thing is to recognize that just because most organizations are not perfect does not mean that they could not be, at least briefly, if only in some areas. We can all improve things, even if we can only improve our particular corner.

It is inevitable when proposing better ways to do things that some aspects are emphasized more than others. You may, if you have a marketing background, consider that the brands – both consumer and employer versions – are the most important aspect to get right as those values and qualities are what drive the rest of the organization's efforts in the long term. If you came up through a management school you may consider that strong and focused leadership is the key characteristic of well-engaged organizations because the tone of inter-employee relationships comes from the very top and filters down, filling every corner and hidden backwater. If you have a media bias you may think that because most corporate programmes fail due to lack of clear communication, getting the media and the messages right is what will deliver the best-engaged organization. A psychology major may support the view that behaviour-driven recognition of tasks well done will reinforce those behaviours to a much greater degree and much more efficiently than any slick piece of promotion.

Of course, all of these are true... and none of them are true, if carried out in isolation. Human beings are complex creatures with reactions and behaviours that can only be predicted in a broad brush way, as will be obvious if you try to allow for the variables of what happens on a daily basis in a large organization by introducing a considered employee or partner programme. When you add the multinational dimension of a global organization, all your channel partners and all your unpaid advocates, the variables run into the billions.

It is comforting to discover a possible 'new way' to deal with age-old people problems, but at best they are refinements of what you already know from being a consumer. Treat consumers well and they and their friends will buy from you again. Treat them badly and you will go out of business. When it comes to work, treat people who work for you well and they will repay you with loyalty and efficiency over the long term. Treat people badly and they and their families will walk away. This is what we mean by managing strategic brand engagement.

The journey from disengagement to engagement, in the context of an organization, is one of taking a handful of related, positive steps and seeing where it leads. There will be a lot of adapting, amending and re-engineering to be done. No two workforces are exactly the same, even over time. There are always leavers and joiners and no two human beings are exactly the same. But the principles of better engagement and reducing disengagement remain. The hard thing, of course, is to do it consistently, in line with your organizational values, over many years, with enthusiasm.

The crucial role of the manager

A national study by Dale Carnegie Training (Lipman, 2013) placed the number of 'fully engaged' employees at 29 per cent, and 'disengaged' employees at 26 per cent – meaning nearly three-quarters of employees are not fully engaged (aka productive). The number one factor the study cited as influencing engagement and disengagement was 'relationship with immediate supervisor'.

Disengagement starts at the team leader level in most organizations, so effective strategies to re-engage with the missing contributors to the corporate good need to focus on managers first of all, supported by the CEO to lend it legitimacy and urgency. Disengagement does not have to be the normal default and most people would prefer to be engaged, given the choice.

Finally, if this the beginning of a new era in improving organizational performance, what does the future hold for engagement initiatives and how sustainable will such programmes be? This is discussed in the next chapter.

The future of strategic brand engagement

14

> *The complexity of the corporation derives from the need to find the right balance between precise and encompassing values, autonomy, and accountability of the board, and engagement with and exposure to third parties.*
>
> **(MAYER, 2013)**

Colin Mayer, Professor of Management Studies at the Said Business School, Oxford, probably did not mean 'engagement' in the sense of a conscious programme of organizational values communication. But the point of needing to recognize that stakeholders outside the organization now have a view about how an organization behaves internally is well made. Social media will ensure an organization's performance reputation will be in the public eye. In the Jetblue example in Chapter 10 we discovered that it only takes a handful of dissatisfied customers to cause an organization considerable embarrassment and loss of significant profits. Strategic brand engagement is all about acknowledging that in the future it will not be enough simply to interact internally with your employees with as little cost and communication as possible... and then hope for the best. Organizations need to treat engagement as a holistic project that affects all its audiences, not just those who work directly for them.

Society and industry have moved on from the days of the implicit promise of a job for life, even in the public sector. This is a major change in working life and as significant as other paradigm shifts that have shaped the way we do business together as societies in the 21st century. Britain's industrial revolution of the 18th century, which created mass production and large employee communities, changed the world and how it created value and did business. The invention of the telephone and commercial flying in the early 20th century accelerated the process of creating economies of scale, with global markets, previously unknown, for all kinds of everyday products. The adoption of the internet by commercial and public sector organizations in the 1990s not only changed organizational processes but created new types of global business models that were unheard of and, in fact, impossible to operate in a pre-internet environment.

But people make organizations truly successful, not processes and technology. The financial challenges and systemic banking failures from 2007 onwards in the developed economies begged the question as to whether 'the market' has now gone too far and that national organizations, multinationals and even governments are no longer in control of their own destinies. When economies go flat for so long, questions are asked about basic issues, such as trust, ethics, morality and the role of the corporation as part of a wider, modern society.

A survey of 34 directors of US Fortune 200 companies in 2010 by Loizos Heracleous, Professor of Strategy at Warwick Business School, revealed a startling finding: 31 of them would cut down a mature forest or release a dangerous, unregulated toxin into the environment to increase corporate earnings (Heracleous, 2010). Double- and triple-dip recessions and similar economic anomalies strongly suggest that we should do more this time than simply tinker with the economic engine, yet again. Perhaps the people dimension needs addressing properly?

Joined-up engagement

The time for serious brand engagement has come if organizations are going to retain the trust of employees and the wider community as both media and markets fragment into ever smaller niche areas. But it has to go further than just another HR campaign to grab briefly the attention of multitasking employees who have their day jobs to do as well as complying with whatever policy change you want them to include this quarter. The sweeping changes in communication that mobile telephony and tablet technology have ushered in have meant that job-holders are now running their social lives concurrently with their professional obligations, often using the same devices. Part-time and working-from-home options mean that the traditional bonds between the organization and people who work for it have diminished to the extent that the old ways of exerting pressure to comply through co-ercion, whether gentle or heavy-handed, may no longer be relevant.

Organizations may have become ever more global but employees have become ever more 'local' in their outlook in terms of their lives, their time and their loyalties. Generation Y does not buy into the idea of total dedica-tion to the work ethic. They have a life outside the organizational structure and are comfortable organizing that life while simultaneously working for an organization, thanks to devices technology. This does not mean organ-izations are being cheated: it is simply a new reality that they need to adapt to and work with. Organizations now have to earn the right to take some of an employee's time rather than expect it to be 100 per cent as a contractual obligation. The firm now has to compete to be noticed.

Engaging with the workforce of the future

People often have more in common with consumer brands and their online 'friends' than they do with who they work for. Employers are in competition for their employees' time rather than just in competition with their business sector rivals. They have to compete for hourly attention with Google, iTunes and Expedia in the workplace. In former times, organizing your social life was something you did when you got home; now, thanks to technology, work and home life is a continuum.

Commercial brand values are clearly understood by employees when they buy products and services. Even children know that advertisements are designed to appeal to them (or to their parents) and that claims of honesty and reliability have to be looked at critically. Marketing principles and techniques are no longer a black art that only the 'hidden persuaders' under-stand. Consumers know the game that is being played.

In the future employers and organizations will need to create, adjust and refine their employer brand to be able to compete for employee time and share of mind in the same way that consumer goods compete for purchasing decisions. They need to change their brand in response to employee and channel partner perceptions – and in a timely fashion or they will lose out to other employers.

Great employee expectations

Employees will expect their leaders to behave in accordance with the principles of strategic brand engagement. Leaders will need to be authentic in their behaviour, not just pay lip-service to corporate values. They need to be trusted at all levels. They need to show a positive attitude and they need to be in dialogue with their employees about changes at all times rather than simply imposing those changes from on high, once a year.

Employees will assume organizations they want to work for will treat them professionally when it comes to communicating the employer brand, explaining values, consulting them about changes and measuring feedback honestly. Just like with consumer products they will know that the message they receive may change if they are part of a different employee community and that one promotional employer claim does not suit all employee or channel partner markets. They will be wise to the tone of voice and any phrases that try to obscure the true situation. If the organization does not tell the truth, it will be found out and very quickly, such is the transparency of the internet and social media these days.

The wider brand engagement community

For an employer brand to work effectively it needs to project itself to the wider community of business partners, advisers, ambassadors and advocates, not just its existing 'customers'. But these groups need to receive a coherent message that is in line with corporate values and very much on brand. Anything less looks unprofessional and careless: it suggests the organization is unable to think in a straight line or with any authenticity.

Employees and advocates will be using open access social networking media to run their everyday lives. Employers need to be aware that the standards of social networking transactions, in terms of ethics, branding and behaviour, will be the same as for when interacting with the organization, so there is no point in having old-style, militaristic, command-and-control rules for organizational life when the real world operates in a more relaxed, open and collaborative way. The 30-year-olds coming through to positions of supervisory power are already familiar with the digital age – they will have experienced no other world – so organizations need to adapt and trade up to the new platforms. Paper diaries, posters and notebooks are inefficient and one-dimensional, offering little option to share and discuss. They belong to the era of private information and the closed shop of outmoded organizational power.

The availability of cheap and flexible data storage and usage systems means there is no excuse now for bland, broad recognition and reward schemes that take no account of individual circumstances. Remuneration can be personalized to the granular level whether that is basic pay, performance rewards or loyalty benefits. What's more, changes should be accommodated at will, if beneficial to employees, rather than annually simply for the convenience of the organization and its vendors.

Engaging with the disengaged

In general about 60 per cent of the employees of well-managed, well-resourced organizations are engaged at present (see Chapter 2). When an organization reaches the dizzy heights of 75 or 80 per cent, champagne corks pop. There is no reason why average engagement scores should not be in the low 90s or more. In the pre-internet era the convenient excuse for why not was that getting the message out to every individual was both time-consuming and often broad brush. With the capability now to tailor messages down to the individual level and receive virtually instant response, there is no reason why employees cannot be fully engaged for most of the time they are at work.

It is less easy to get full commitment from channel partners and advocates simply because their economic ties are less binding. But if Amazon can offer millions of consumers the books they actually want to buy on what seems like a personal recommendation based on previous buying habits, it is only a question of time before organizational partners will receive tailored messages that resonate with their own team rather than having to think how this organizational message could be applied to their own local situation. The resources to do this already exist in terms of line management and access to policy information. Where it often fails at the individual level is good communication tools and, to be honest, remembering to keep team members informed in a way they will relate to. Quarterly financial headlines are not the answer.

Engagement and loyalty

In Chapter 2 we looked at the economic reasons for treating engagement strategies now as a priority – everyone benefits, especially the shareholders. To some extent the argument assumes that most organizations have employees who travel to work to fixed locations. When commentators first started writing about the potential effects of the internet on working life, remote working was hailed as the model for future organizations. The attractive and compelling idea was that 'in the future' most people would have a portfolio working week, largely based at home, and that a typical jobholder would interact with his or her colleagues over the 'net' and only work a few hours a day for any one employer. Just like the futurist myth of vitamin pills being substituted for food and space travel for all, it has not come to pass. The vast majority of workers still travel to a fixed location to work and the best work is done by being in close human contact with groups of other people. Although flexible working has risen, it is still not the way the majority of the workforce earns a living today.

For that reason effective engagement, in the main, will still be mostly about fixed location programmes for large numbers of people who share common corporate values and goals. But the introduction of channel partners and advocates into the engagement mix suggests that, through corporate social media, engagement can be promoted in a much more timely, informal and widely dispersed way than before. But rather than simply let it happen, the process can be engineered in such a way that 'good organizations' can control the communication of their values and create loyalty beyond the confines of the bricks and glass of fixed locations and the gossip around the water cooler. It can be actively managed in the ether rather than just passively promoted.

Get a plan

Employees are pretty smart. They are like you and me. They can spot a turkey from a long way off. In Jim Haudan's entertaining and insightful book, *The Art of Engagement* (2008), he tells it like it is and describes what a frontline associate of an organization he had dealings with said about senior management:

> I used to see complete incompetence. We got all this flavour-of-the-month stuff.
> We figured that leaders were trying to please each other or someone other than

us – the people who do the work. We just assumed that leaders couldn't agree on what came next... they're just not very good at helping us understand things.

If senior executives are good at anything it should be planning skills. They have usually had about 20 or even 30 years to practise, so they should be better at it than most people. If 'strategic' means anything it should mean you have a plan. I wrote my first business book almost 20 years ago about incentives and put together a simple diagram for 'performance improvement' which is the agenda for any internal change initiative; see Figure 14.1.

FIGURE 14.1   The performance improvement model

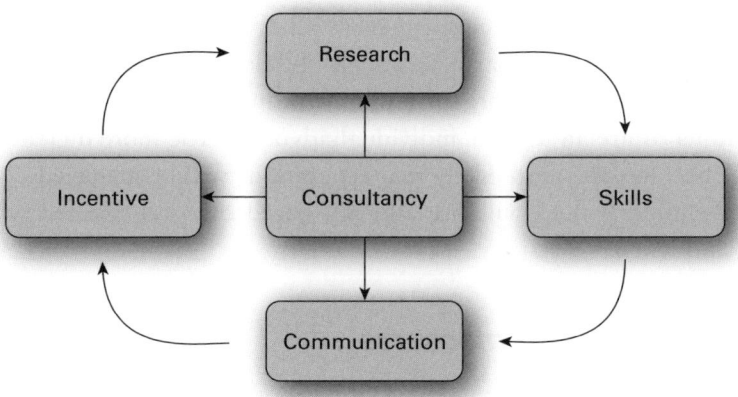

It suggests that before you do anything, you should do some research – it may be formal and cost a fortune or it may be undertaken by your team and cost almost nothing. But do some. You would be surprised how many organizations launch into major change initiatives on the whim of an article the CEO saw in business magazine that may have no relevance at all to the organization at that time or its trade sector.

You should examine the skills of those who will be required to manage the change. If brand engagement is a mix of hard-nosed HR calculations and marketing communication skills, does your team and the internal management infrastructure know enough technically about how to get leverage from any activity you may put into place?

What incentives are you going to put in place to encourage change? It's an old saying in business that what gets rewarded gets done. It does not have to be life-changing: often token rewards and lots of recognition are powerful enough. An incentive, however small, signals to employees and the channel that this is an initiative you want to be taken seriously, not just a 'nice-to-have'.

Once these steps have been gone through, go through them again and again at every stage so that you are constantly questioning whether you have asked enough questions, got the right skills, communicated the change effectively and offered participants a reason to change their behaviour. If any of these steps are missing or poorly addressed it is likely your engagement ambitions will also fall short. That's a plan – so your brand engagement activity is now 'strategic'.

In the final analysis brand engagement is all about loyalty from both paid and unpaid preferential partners and it should not matter whether you are employed by the same organization, work in the same building, work in the channel or are an unpaid, individual advocate. The more digital organizations become, the more likely that reputations will be managed digitally and stakeholder values will rise and fall based on who tweeted what to whom and when.

Public engagement measures

In Chapter 2 we discussed the financial reasons why engagement is a good idea for any organization. In October 2013 the Enterprise Engagement Alliance launched the EEA Good Company Stock Index (GCSI) in the United States to draw attention to the compelling connection between the organization's relationships with customers, employees and communities and its subsequent performance in the stock market. Initially it will track 30 companies with high Good Company scores, comparing them with low scores and the S&P average. In time it is hoped that this index will be one of the important benchmarking factors that both investors and employees will use to rate leading organizations, not only in the United States but across the developed world. The EEA has also developed a number of training and development products for engagement professionals which are well worth investigating as a formal means to accrediting your organization's managers with the requisite skills to do the engagement job effectively; see the 'Online resources' section in the next chapter.

Bridging the generation gap

There is no doubt that a major factor driving the need for better engagement is the different ways Baby Boomers and Generation Y use communication channels and media. With the raising of official retirement ages for Baby Boomers and the proliferation of social media channels used by Generation Y, there is scope for a disconnect in communication within organizations.

Older workers are not retiring anytime soon so organizations that ignore the generation gap and the differences in how they communicate with each other may suffer. Stroud and Walker (2013) comment on a survey by the Boston Consulting Group of populations in the United States, UK, Japan, Canada, France, Germany and Italy in 2010: 'In 2010 there were 375 million over-60s... In the next 20 years, by the end of 2030, this number will be 695 million.' Those in positions of power – primarily the Baby Boomers – who have not done so already will have to get comfortable with social media if they want to engage fully with their younger, more media-aware workforces.

The engagement VP

So if engagement is going to be one of the crucial metrics of successful organizations, someone will have to take responsibility for its delivery. It will be the Engagement VP's role to try and control this whole process rather than be its victim. He or she will have to be a hybrid of existing HR and marketing VPs who know how to save money but also how to spend it. He or she will have to be able to research and recognize a trend as well as create new trends that are beneficial to the organization and its brand values. He or she will be able to be critical about how the organization's values get translated into the many social media now available and be able to manage the reputation of the organization, both internally and externally, online and offline.

Above all, the Engagement VP will need to gain and maintain trust from many internal and external groups in the same way that a successful brand builds consumer trust over many years through brand performance. Better and persistent engagement requires organizational building skills and marketing skills to an equal degree. Not an easy portfolio. But the brand future you envision for your organization cannot be left alone to simply evolve. The Engagement VP and his or her team will have to make it happen.

So, over to you. Are you happy with the way your brand engages your employees to improve their performance? If not, you may need to do some research. If you are proud of your employee engagement scores, how well do these scores compare with the scores of your sales people and channel distributors? Have you thought about your CSR programme and whether your advocates and volunteers are in the engagement loop and whether they fully understand your values and how they can be used to engage better with consumers? There is still plenty for you to be doing when it comes to engagement.

BIBLIOGRAPHY AND ONLINE RESOURCES

Ansoff, H (1981) *Corporate Strategy*, Penguin, London

Barrow, S and Mosley, R (2005) *The Employer Brand*, Wiley, Chichester

Buckingham, I (2008) *Brand Engagement*, Palgrave Macmillan, Basingstoke

Chandler, A D Jnr (1962) *Strategy and Structure*, MIT Press, Cambridge, MA

Chartered Institute of Personnel and Development (2012) *Employer Brand Factsheet*, September, CIPD, London, www.cipd.co.uk

Chartered Management Institute (2012) *Bad Management is Harming UK PLC*, introductory remarks: www.managers.org.uk

Collins, J C and Porras, J I (1994) *Built to Last*, HarperBusiness Essentials series, HarperCollins, New York

Collins, J C and Porras, J I (1996) Building your company's vision, *Harvard Business Review*, September

Cook, S (2008) *The Essential Guide to Employee Engagement*, Kogan Page, London

Coupland, D C (1991) *Generation X: Tales for an accelerated culture*, St Martin's Press, New York

Conyngham Performance Group (2012) *White Paper: Why channel partner engagement (and partners in general) are important*, May, Enterprise Engagement Alliance website: www.enterpriseengagement.org

Deye, D (2012) David Ogilvy: The danger of discounting, *Brand Strategy Insider* website, 4 May

Drucker, P (2011) *Managing for Results*, Butterworth Heinemann, Oxford

Entec Corporation (2012) Employee Toolkit series: *Understanding Employee Disengagement*, 28 December, www.employeesurveytoolkit.com

Fisher, J G (2008) *How to Run Successful Employee Incentive Schemes*, 3rd edn, Kogan Page, London

Fleming, J and Apslund, J (2005) Gallup's Human Sigma model, *Harvard Business Review*, July/August

Ghiel, W and LePla, F J (2012) *Create a Brand that Inspires*, Author House, Bloomington, IN

Golovinski, S (2011) *Event 3.0*, www.newtonstrand.com

Green, C (2012) Why trust is the new core of leadership, *Forbes Woman*, 4 March

Handy, C (1999) *Understanding Organizations*, 4th edn, Penguin, London

Haudan, J (2008) *The Art of Engagement*, McGraw-Hill, New York

Hay Group Australia (2012) *White Paper: Why does engagement matter to CEOs?* www.haygroup.com/au

Heracleous, L (2010) The myth of shareholder capitalism, *Harvard Business Review*, April

Hewett, D and Arshad, R (2013) Call to arms, *Argent*, 40, Spring

Ind, N (2012) *Living the Brand*, 3rd edn, Kogan Page, London

Jensen, M C and Murphy, K J (1990) CEO incentives: it's not how much you pay, but how, *Harvard Business Review*, May

Kohler, H (1997) *Economic Systems and Human Welfare: A global survey*, South-Western, Cincinnati, OH

Kouzes, J and Posner, B (2009) Transformational leadership model in practice: The case of Jordanian schools, *Journal of Leadership Education*, 7 (3)

Lipman, V (2013) Why are so many employees disengaged? *Forbes*, January

Macey, W, Schneider, B, Barbara, K and Young, S (2009) *Employee Engagement*, Wiley Blackwell, Chichester

McGregor, D (1960) *The Human Side of Enterprise*, McGraw Hill, New York

Maxwell, C (2013) Blogging for business, *The Director*, April

Mayer, C (2013) *Firm Commitment*, Oxford University Press, Oxford

Nayar, V (2010) *Employees First, Customers Second*, Harvard Business Press, Boston, MA

Neumeier, M (2006) *The Brand Gap*, Pearson Education, Berkeley, CA

Nicholson, N (2013) *The 'I' of Leadership*, Wiley, Chichester

Olins, W (2007) *On Brand*, Thames & Hudson, London

Phelps, G (2004) What the big picture doesn't show, *Gallup Business Journal*, June, www.businessjournal.gallup.com

Porter, M (2004) *Competitive Strategy: Techniques for analyzing industries and competitors*, Free Press, New York

Sartain, L and Schumann, M (2006) *Brand From the Inside*, Jossey-Bass, San Francisco, CA

Schweyer, A (2009) White paper, Enterprise Engagement Alliance, www.enterpriseengagement.org

Smythe, J (2007) *The CEO: Chief Engagement Officer*, Gower Publishing, Aldershot

Solis, B (2011) *Engage!* Wiley, New Jersey

Stroud, D and Kim Walker, K (2013) *Marketing to the Ageing Consumer*, Palgrave Macmillan, Basingstoke

Weinberg, T (2009) *The New Community Rules*, O'Reilly Media, Sebastopol, CA

Williams, A and Mullins, R (2008) *The Handbook of Field Marketing*, Kogan Page, London

Willock, R (2005) Employer branding is key in fight for talent, *Personnel Today*, 17 May: www.personneltoday.com

Online resources

Engagement Strategies Magazine: www.sellingcommunications.com
Enterprise Engagement Alliance: www.enterpriseengagement.org
Experiential Marketing Forum: www.experientialforum.com
Fisher Moy International: www.fmigroup.co.uk
Gallup: www.gallup.com
Incentive Marketing Association (United States): www.incentivemarketing.org

INDEX

(*italics* indicates a figure in the text)